IDEAS AND IDEALS

IDEAS and IDEALS

By
HASTINGS RASHDALL
D.D., D.C.L., D.Litt., F.B.A.
Sometime Dean of Carlisle

Selected by
H. D. A. MAJOR, D.D., F.S.A.
Principal of Ripon Hall, Oxford
and
F. L. CROSS, M.A., B.Sc.
Librarian of Pusey House

Essay Index Reprint Series

BOOKS FOR LIBRARIES PRESS
FREEPORT, NEW YORK

First Published 1928
Reprinted 1968

LIBRARY OF CONGRESS CATALOG CARD NUMBER:

68-16970

PRINTED IN THE UNITED STATES OF AMERICA

CONTENTS

PREFACE

THE cordial reception accorded by reviewers and readers to *Principles and Precepts* (now in its second edition) has encouraged its editors to compile another volume from the papers of the late Dean of Carlisle.

Unlike *Principles and Precepts* the present volume is not homiletic, but consists of papers and essays dealing in a succinct and lucid manner with important problems in theology, ethics, and metaphysics. Readers who are not conversant with Dr. Rashdall's great works, *The Idea of the Atonement in Christian Theology,* and *The Theory of Good and Evil,* may find the substance of his teaching in this small volume.

We wish to express our thanks to the Council of the British Academy for permission to republish Paper XII, and to the Rev. John Carter, sometime editor of *The Economic Review,* for permission to republish Papers II, III, IV. Papers I, VII, VIII are reprinted from *The Modern Churchman.*

Should the circulation of this volume warrant it, we shall be happy to compile a third volume from the rich storehouse of the Dean's literary remains.

H. D. A. M.
F. L. C.

IDEAS AND IDEALS

I

THE VALIDITY OF RELIGIOUS EXPERIENCE [1]

WHEN a phrase becomes a " blessed word," it becomes a very dangerous thing. It is hardly a paradox to say that, in the region of philosophy, a truth which has become a catchword or badge of a particular school or tendency is in a fair way to pass into a falsity. The danger is certainly not less when the subject is one which concerns religion. In large circles " religious experience " is the " blessed word " of the moment; and that word is now employed with a laxity which tends —to say the least of it—to intellectual confusion.

Of course, nobody denies the existence of religious experience as a psychological phenomenon. Nobody denies the existence of religious ideas, religious belief, religious emotion. And the present fashion of treating these religious phenomena—whether those which are commonly accounted normal or those which are, more or less, abnormal—as subjects of serious inquiry, as things which cannot be simply disposed of by the use of such terms as insanity or hysteria, hallucination or neurosis, may be welcomed. But when religious people eagerly jump at the present willingness of psychologists to deal with such subjects in a serious spirit, when they let themselves talk about dismissing logic or metaphysic as the obsolete delusions of an older world, and appeal to psychology as the new, up-to-date science which is going to place religion upon an unassailable foundation, they forget that psychology has got nothing to do with the truth of religious beliefs—that is to say, of any beliefs which assert anything beyond the fact that such and such a

[1] A paper read at the Churchmen's Union Conference at Girton College, Cambridge, 1918. Reprinted from *The Modern Churchman*, vol. viii, pp. 302–15.

person has such and such a subjective experience. From the psychological point of view, the fact that Luther had an experience of seeing the devil and that Kant had an experience of duty are precisely on the same level. If a modern inquirer comes to the conclusion that Luther's belief in the objective presence of the devil at the Wartburg in 1521 was a mere delusion, while Kant's belief in an objective experience of the moral law was a true belief, it is not as a psychologist that he draws the distinction. When a confused thinker constructs a syllogism with an undisturbed middle or some such logical fallacy in it and is quite satisfied with his conclusion, it is not the psychologist who can pronounce his inference false. Psychology knows nothing of the difference between false syllogisms and valid ones. There is a sense in which all religious beliefs must rest upon the facts of psychology, since the most important data which we have for constructing our theory of the universe are the facts about the spiritual nature of man. Human sensations, thoughts, emotions, volitions, are all psychological facts; but if, upon the basis of any of these mental phenomena, we construct a theory as to the nature of God or of the universe as a whole, we do not do so as psychologists, and it is not psychology which can tell us whether our belief is true or false. The notion that a religion can be constructed which involves no logic and no metaphysic is, I venture to think, simply a delusion. I think it is well to put this point clearly, but, of course, it does not by itself settle anything as to the validity of the appeal to religious experience as a source of knowledge. This appeal seems to be made in a number of different senses, a few of which—I have only time to deal with a few—I will now attempt to distinguish.

(1) In the mouths of some philosophers the assertion appears to mean that religion is not concerned with objective truth or falsehood at all. Religious experience is not only the foundation of religion: it *is*

8

religion, and the whole of it. When Mr. Herbert Bradley says that "the man who demands a reality more solid than that of the religious consciousness seeks he knows not what," he appears to mean that religious experience is all that the religious man wants, no matter how little any reality beyond the experience corresponds to it. It would be impossible to deal with this view thoroughly without discussing Mr. Bradley's system as a whole. It is perhaps sufficient to say that it is a view which will not satisfy most religious persons—least of all the persons who use the kind of language about religious experience with which I am now chiefly concerned. They believe that religious experience authorises them to make certain statements about the objective nature of the universe.

(2) There are persons who by the appeal to religious experience seem to mean that the fact that they have certain religious emotions warrants their asserting certain things about the object of such emotions. This notion seems to be so extravagant that I do not quite see how to set about refuting it. Savages have felt all sorts of emotions towards all sorts of deities: does this emotion prove the objective existence of all the Pantheons of all the polytheistic religions? And surely it is quite arbitrary to contend that, though the emotion does not prove the existence of all or any of these polytheistic deities, it does prove that some deity exists. And even if this could be admitted, it would be no very valuable discovery unless we know something about that deity—whether he is to be invested with the character attributed by Manasseh to Molech, or with that which the Jewish prophets ascribed to Jehovah, or with the attributes which are ascribed by Christians to the God of Christianity. I cannot see how a subjective emotion can prove the existence of its object. Moreover, the emotion itself implies an already existing belief. The intellectual belief cannot be due merely to the emotion: however the belief be arrived at (whether by tradition, imagination, authority, in-

9

ference true or false), the emotion implies that the intellectual belief is already there. Destroy that belief, and it goes. Let the savage chief be convinced by the arguments of the missionary that his idols are silver and gold, the work of men's hands, and he no longer feels the old awe, the old fear, the old trust when he approaches them. It is the same with the higher types of religious emotion. The biographies of those who have given up the religion of their childhood are full of testimony to that effect. Renan, as the famous Professor of the Collège de France, certainly no longer experienced the awe with which he had knelt before the host in the Cathedral of Tréguier or even the awe with which he had then regarded the moral law.

(3) With others, the appeal to religious experience as the foundation of religious belief amounts simply to the assertion that there is such a thing as an immediate or intuitive or *a priori* knowledge of God's existence. It is impossible to discuss the subject without making the avowal that (so far as I can analyse my own thoughts) I have no such intuitive knowledge myself. When I have intuitive knowledge, I find it impossible to doubt. I could not possibly doubt that two and two make four, that two straight lines cannot enclose a space, that nothing can begin to be without a cause, that certain premisses necessitate certain conclusions.[1] But the existence of God, unfortunately, I find it quite possible to doubt, and, when doubts arise in my mind, I have to meet them by arguments or rational considerations of one kind or another. At an early age my belief was, of course, due solely to authority, suggestion, environment; the fact that I have retained—of course, with some modification in my conception of God—the belief of my childhood is due (so far as I can see) to the influence of these rational considerations. Knowledge of that kind is not

[1] I cannot here deal with the highly technical argument of those who deny *any* "isolated" intuition in the sense of a full and final validity, not liable to correction or modification from the rest of our knowledge.

immediate or intuitive. I do not know of any sort of immediate knowledge, or anything which can be at all plausibly called immediate knowledge, which bears the least resemblance to this alleged immediate knowledge of another spiritual being. It may be doubted whether even my knowledge of myself can properly be called immediate, in the strict sense of the word, since it is only by reflecting on what is implied in many successive states of mind that I construct the notion of a continuous self. I will not say that my knowledge of myself is an " inference "; it may better be described as an " intellectual construction." But certainly my knowledge of other people's existence is a matter of inference. No philosopher has ever doubted this, so far as I know, till quite recently, and even now the contrary view has hardly been asserted outside Oxford, and no systematic defence of so paradoxical an opinion has ever yet been produced even in Oxford.

The fact that I, personally, am conscious of no such immediate knowledge of God would, no doubt, by itself, prove little. But I am sure that the vast majority of my fellow-men, including the most religious of them, are in the same state of mind. Missionaries do not find that they can assume a knowledge of God in their hearers; they have to prove it by arguments—good, bad, or indifferent. The arguments may often be " pragmatical," but they are, none the less, arguments. They get no converts till they are thought to have proved it. Whole populations are without the idea of one God; some savages can hardly be said to believe in many gods. Educated Chinamen or Japanese, we are told, do not usually believe either in one God or in many. Individuals among ourselves, who are brought up without " religious education," do not commonly possess this belief. If I confine myself to Christians, I read Fathers, Schoolmen, modern theologians, without ever coming across a single trace of such a claim to such immediate knowledge. I do not say there are no exceptions. The great masters of philosophical thought, including the most theistic, never suggest such a notion. It is equally absent from the thought of what I may call the professional meta-physicians, and from that of men of essentially religious genius. Martineau's belief in God was reached by way of inference—chiefly from our experience of causality in our voluntary action, which is extended by inference to the cause of all phenomena. Newman declares that the existence of God and of self constituted for him the two great certainties; but he declares also that his reason for believing in God is the existence of his own moral consciousness. A belief for which a reason, a " because," can be given, is not immediate. In truth the claim to an immediate knowledge of God was almost confined to the small group of writers of different ages who are called mystics, and by them this knowledge is usually supposed to be obtainable only by a long course of meditation. The mystics have always been few. The great religious leaders of mankind, the main currents of religious thought, the vast mass of believers in any religion, or, at all events, in any definitely theistic religion, have not been mystics in any strict sense of that very ambiguous and much-abused word. The average religious man equally disclaims any such immediate consciousness. The simple Christian declares that his belief rests on faith. Whatever faith means for him, it certainly does not mean the same thing as sight.[1]

These considerations would, no doubt, by themselves not disprove the validity of an intuitive knowledge of God in the comparatively few persons who, with full knowledge of its meaning, actually make the claim. A self-evident truth does not necessarily mean a truth which is evident to everybody. As a rule, indeed, a

[1] No one has insisted more than the Editor of *The Challenge* upon the importance of religious experience; yet, in an article of August 9, 1918, I read: " Faith is not knowledge, and its spiritual value depends upon the fact that it contains a real hazard."

belief which is really self-evident is found, or is capable of being awakened by a sufficient amount of education and reflection, in the normal human consciousness; but there is nothing inconceivable in the conception of an intellectual insight, or, if you please, a super-intellectual insight, which is possessed by very few persons. And I should be quite prepared to attach great importance to the testimony of such persons if I found that there was any agreement in what they tell us about God. But, in point of fact, there is none. I do not know a single proposition about God which is not asserted by some mystics to be self-evidently true, by others to be self-evidently false. I put aside such claims to immediate knowledge as extend to the whole content of traditional religion. One does find, of course, men not wholly illiterate who claim to know intuitively the fact of the Virgin Birth, or the truth of the Christian Creed as a whole. But even if we confine ourselves to the more philosophical kind of mystic, who does not claim any immediate knowledge of historical facts, we find the flattest contradictions. The Christian mystic of anything approaching an orthodox type usually asserts that God is a Person or a Spirit; many a Hindoo mystic is equally sure that He is not personal. The Christian mystic thinks of Him as righteous and loving; for the Hindoo mystic, or some Hindoo mystics, it is a degradation to ascribe moral qualities to the Deity; morality for them is a purely human and very contemptible affair of no cosmic significance. God is beyond good and evil. The Buddhist mystic's insight may extend beyond this; sometimes he is agnostic, or may even know immediately the non-existence of anything which the Western mind could recognise as God at all.

It is admitted by the late Professor William James, who is largely responsible for the present disposition to rely upon intuitions which the philosopher admits that he does not himself possess, that, when these intuitions differ, the differences must be held to cancel

13

one another. The residual creed, which remains after this cancelling-out process has been performed, is surely something so vague and exiguous, even upon James's own showing, that it does not really seem to make much difference whether one believes it or not. The most that it comes to, according to his own showing, is that there is some consciousness beyond that of the individual. But even that is, I think, more than would be accepted by all the claimants to immediate knowledge. For consciousness is not a universally admitted predicate of Deity as conceived of in the East, and, indeed, predicates are just what the most profound philosophical mystics have denied to the Deity. His nature can only be expressed by negations. In fact, if this cancelling process is fairly carried out, nothing will remain but the famous creed of Parmenides—that Being is, and not Being is not. And, indeed, if we turn to some of the mystical utterances, this difference, too, must be transcended; and then nothing will remain but the assertion that the mystic is conscious of that which may be indifferently described as Being or as Not-being. To some, perhaps, such an abstraction must be an acceptable object of worship. For myself, I would rather have a slight probability of the existence of something like the Christian Deity than an intuitive certainty of this kind. It will be observed that no moral qualities are even claimed for this residual Deity of Professor James.

Are we then to say that the appeal to immediate intuitions, or what appear to the person experiencing them to be such, is worthless? Far from it. I am sorry that from the nature of the case I have been obliged to make my argument chiefly negative and destructive: I have no time to develop what I believe to be the real basis for religious belief beyond saying that, for me, belief in God rests upon the sort of arguments which, in a developed and systematic form, are to be found in the writings of theistic philosophers and philosophical theologians. What amount of truth or validity there is in the various lines of thought which have at various times constituted the actual grounds of religious belief, I must not attempt to examine; I must be content with barely suggesting in the vaguest possible way the elements of truth which I can recognise in this attempt to base religious belief upon the appeal to the apparently spontaneous and immediate deliverances of the religious consciousness, whether in the average religious man or in the exceptionally gifted religious natures:

(1) Very often what presents itself to the plain man as a self-evident religious truth is a really rational argument for belief, but one which he has never analysed and perhaps could not analyse. There is in it an element of inference, which may be quite good and valid inference (though of course it is not so in all cases), but which escapes his own notice. The inference is what is often called " unconscious inference." His immediate certainty may be based upon the appearances of design and intelligence in nature—upon the kind of argument which is put by St. Luke into the mouth of St. Paul at Athens, and which is developed in a more elaborate form by such men as Socrates, Cicero, Thomas Aquinas, Leibniz, Paley, von Hartmann, Lord Haldane, M. Bergson, Mr. Balfour. The mere juxtaposition of these names shows that I do not mean that all forms of the " argument for design " are equally valid, but still they do all represent attempts to get at the real truth which in a confused form is recognised by the " plain man " when he says, " I don't think the world "—by this he means the material world—" can have made itself. It is clear to me that it must have been planned by, or be ruled by, a conscious intelligence." Or, at the bottom of his mind, there may be a vague notion of the superior value of mind to matter and the consequent necessity of thinking of the ultimate nature of things in terms of mind—a line of thought which, if developed, might

lead him to the system of Hegel—one interpretation
of Hegel at least—or of Green or of Professor
Pringle-Pattison. Or, like Newman, he may be im-
pressed with the fact that his own immediate consciousness of duty can only be fully and adequately
explained by the view that moral distinctions are inherent in the mind of God. He may be an unconscious
disciple of Butler or of Kant, of Cudworth or of
Mansel. And so on. The notion that we can construct a religion which is independent of metaphysics
is a delusion. We are all metaphysicians, especially
those who do not know it. There is no sharp line
between the vague and unanalysed thinking of the
plain man or the unphilosophical man of religious
genius and the analysed and thought-out reasonings
or reflections of the philosopher. I have no doubt that
to the mind of a Jewish prophet the existence and the
attributes of Jehovah presented themselves as intuitive
certainties, but that does not exclude the possibility
that his convictions (so far as they were not merely
traditional) rested upon unconscious processes of reflection. There are many fine rhetorical or poetic
passages of the Jewish prophets which might easily be
re-written in the form of a Platonic dialogue, a scholastic *quæstio,* or a page of the most modern philosophy.

(2) Although I do not think there can be said
to be a valid intuition of God, it must be remembered
that many of the premisses unconsciously employed
really are self-evident truths. The most important
of these is the consciousness of moral obligation, which
does, as it seems to me, require the belief in God for its
satisfactory explanation, though I will not say that
a theistic argument can be constructed on this basis
alone, taken in absolute abstraction from all other
elements in our knowledge of the human mind. The
argument from an absolute duty to God generally
involves some assumptions which might conceivably
be disputed, and which it would require other arguments to justify, but at bottom I believe there is no

16

more solid foundation for religious belief than the immediate consciousness of duty.

(3) Sometimes the appeal to religious experience takes the form not so much of a claim to an immediate knowledge of God as of an argument based upon the fact of there being such a thing as religious experience, whether understood as religious emotion or as intellectual belief. The argument then becomes something like a modernised version of the old argument *ex consensu gentium,* which, in the light of modern knowledge, must of course be re-stated in a form which does not imply an absolutely universal belief in a god or gods. Or the implicit argument may rely upon the improbability of our having been created with emotions, aspirations, tendencies to think (if not actual thoughts), the adequate satisfaction of which is denied by the constitution of the universe—a line of thought with which Mr. Balfour has made us very familiar. I should be far from denying the value of such a line of argument, but I do not think it possesses any very great cogency except upon a certain assumption. That assumption is the belief that the universe is ultimately rational. If the universe were really a mindless machine churning out as mere epi-phenomena or accidental by-products all the conscious experiences which we call thoughts, volitions, emotions, etc., I do not know that a few more unsatisfied desires and aspirations would be any harder to account for than the evolutionary process as a whole or the normal workings of the normal mind. The strength of the argument is really derived from the various lines of thought which lead us to believe that the universe *is* rational. And when we have once got this premiss, we are pretty well independent of this appeal to the argument based upon the universality of religion in the many or the strength of the religious emotions and beliefs in the most religious natures, though I should cordially recognise its comfirmatory value. Religion is one of the things which are most reasonably accounted for on

the theistic hypothesis, but it is by no means the only one.

(4) No doubt the aversion which religious minds often feel for the notion that belief in God is really due to an inference springs from the desire to feel that we may in prayer and religious communion come into immediate contact with God—that we may speak with God face to face as a man speaketh with his friend. If we admit that our knowledge of the human friend has equally in it an element which the logician must recognise as an inference, and even an inference which amounts (in strict logic) only to an enormous balance of probability, I do not think that there is any real substance in the objection. The warmth of friendship or family affection was surely never dimmed by the admission that after all one's knowledge of one's nearest relation or one's best friend involves an inference. So it may be with the soul's approach to God; the conviction that prayer puts us into a real relation to God may be none the less well-grounded, because the belief in God, like the belief in a friend, involves inference. I may add that this does not involve the corollary that God's knowledge of us is only inferential. It was only in another life that St. Paul expected to know, even as we are already known.

(5) There is nothing in the theory that valid knowledge of God is inferential which need prevent us thinking of religious knowledge, emotion—religious experience, if you please, in any of its forms or aspects —as being due to inspiration or revelation. When we have once reached our knowledge of God, then we must regard all sorts of true knowledge—and in an especial sense, all religious knowledge and spiritual insight—as implanted in the human mind by God, as due (in the language of Green) to a partial communication to us of the knowledge which is already perfect in the Divine Mind. A valid inference may be regarded as no less coming from God than an

immediate intuition,[1] though doubtless in the Divine Mind we cannot suppose that there is that distinction between immediate apprehension and knowledge reached by way of inference or reflection, which the partial character of our knowledge imposes upon ourselves.

The prophet of the order of Isaiah is no less a true prophet of God because what present themselves to him as intuitions are really what a prophet of the order of Plato might recognise as an unconscious philosophical argument. But I do not assert that the highest religious ideas of an Isaiah, a St. John, or a St. Paul were necessarily arrived at by any process of inference, however unconscious. I cannot, indeed, with M. Auguste Sabatier, regard a thought as necessarily a divine inspiration just because it is not connected, logically or psychologically, with anything previously in the mind; the ideas of madmen are often equally without traceable antecedents, whether logical or psychological. But when the ideas are there, and we have some other reason for regarding them as true, then we need not hesitate to think of them as coming from the Mind from which all truth proceeds. The apparently spontaneous occurrence of such ideas to certain minds may be one of the ways in which God reveals Himself to mankind. And the same consideration may be applied to the dimmer religious instincts or aspirations or dispositions to believe, which ordinary men, not gifted with any exceptional religious insight, may discover in their own minds. These, too, may be a kind of divine inspiration, just so far as they are actually true ideas. What I have been dealing with is not the existence of, or the value of, such apparently immediate religious ideas, emotions, thoughts, experiences, nor again the strength of conviction which they actually bring to the person who experiences them, but the question of their validity from the point of view

[1] It should be remembered that all inference rests upon certain laws of thought which are themselves self-evident.

of the impartial inquirer. Such an inquirer cannot accept all such ideas of another person as true, no matter how strongly that person may declare the immediacy of his insight or the certainty with which they present themselves to him, because (as I pointed out) they are often contradicted by equally confident assertions on the part of others; and, to me at least, the law of contradiction presents itself as the most certain of all immediate certainties, though there are doubtless mystics who claim to have seen through that delusion as well as others. I hold with St. Paul that, while we should not quench the Spirit nor despise prophesyings, we should prove all things, and only hold fast to that which on reflection presents itself to us as true. Many of the truths which the philosopher may find good grounds for believing may, nevertheless, be such as would have never occurred to him but for the intuitions of the prophet, the poet, the man of religious genius; and yet he is right in demanding some reason for thinking them true. Nor would I deny the reasonableness of attaching great weight to the authority of such gifted personalities in religious matters. The individual may be quite justified in accepting the unproved dicta of the prophet or teacher whom he thinks more likely to be right than himself; belief on authority is perfectly reasonable if we have good grounds for trusting the authority; but when and in so far as I am examining the *ultimate* grounds for belief, I cannot recognise the intuition of God as a valid immediate judgement in the sense in which I do regard my belief in geometrical axioms or in moral obligation as valid immediate judgements. I believe that a knowledge of God is to be reached by way of inference or—to use a term which covers something more than what is usually called logical inference, and which admits, it may be said, some closer approach to immediacy—by a process of reflection. The belief in the existence of God rests upon rational grounds which admit of being stated in an articulate and intelligible way—a way not more inadequate than other ways of expressing thought are inadequate to the reality, or which are only more inadequate because the subject-matter to which they relate is one in which, from the nature of the case, language must always in an exceptional degree be inadequate to the thought, and the thought to the reality. Poet, prophet, and philosopher may equally fail to express fully all the truth that they apprehend, or to state with completeness the grounds upon which that truth rests; but that is a different thing from saying that it rests upon no grounds at all.

The position for which I have contended is one which I believe has the support of nearly all the philosophers, nearly all the theologians, nearly all the great religious minds. Whatever is of value in the testimony of that very small group of men known as mystics need not be ignored or denied because a more analytical mind might discover that their thought too was partly inference or because, when it is not so, such minds demand some rational grounds for accepting what they intuitively pronounce to be true. Do not many at least of the psychologists assure us that a great part of what we think we see with the bodily eye is really inference? Faith was not, it is of the last importance to remember, for men like St. Paul opposed to Reason, but only to Sight.

II

THE RIGHTS OF THE STATE[1]

I PROPOSE in these lectures to be almost entirely theoretical. Having no pretensions to be an economist, I could not attempt to deal with any detailed questions of political economy. Having little practical experience, I should hesitate to put before you any views of mine as to the practical questions of the day. My work at Oxford has familiarised me chiefly with the most theoretical and abstract way of looking at social and political questions. I am far from thinking that technical philosophy can supply any short cut to the solution of practical problems. But you will, I trust, be prepared to recognise that a clear view of fundamental principles is of some value even in the practical conflict with pressing social difficulties. And it is perhaps in helping to some clear view of principles that a dweller in academic groves may have most chance of being of some little use to people who are in a closer contact than himself with the misery of the world and with the practical efforts directed towards its removal. I had better perhaps explain at once that, as I can hardly venture to assume on the part of all my hearers much previous acquaintance with the course of political speculation, I shall have to be somewhat elementary. In the present lecture, at all events, I must confine myself to commonplaces which will, I fear, be a very old story to some of you.

In the history of political thought there have been three, and only three, main theories as to the basis of the duty of political obedience—as to the source, and consequently as to the limits, of the State's authority. They are:

(a) The theory of Divine right.

[1] This and the two papers which follow formed a course of lectures delivered before the London Branch of the Christian Social Union. They are reprinted from *The Economic Review*, vol. vi (1896), pp. 59–75, 166–182, 317–333.

22

(*b*) The social contract theory.

(*c*) The view which I may provisionally call the utilitarian.

1. Firstly, then, there is the theory of Divine right. This is the theory of some among the Fathers who lived under the despotism of the Roman Empire, of the Ghibelline writers of the Middle Ages, and of the Anglican apologists of the Stuarts in the seventeenth century. Of course, whatever be the source of the State's right, every Christian believes that, when that right is established, it can claim a Divine sanction. In that sense all rights and all authority are Divine. By the theory of Divine right I mean only either the theory which holds that the *de facto* sovereign (no matter whether he owes his position to birth, to conquest, or to the Praetorian *émeute* which murdered his predecessor) has an authority which cannot be forfeited by any kind or any amount of misgovernment, or the theory that some particular mode of appointment—whether the choice of an electoral college of princes or descent in the direct eldest male line from Adam—secures this unlimited authority to the legitimate sovereign. Such arbitrary theories could only be supported by the pretence of direct Divine revelation. And of such a pretension it is enough to say that the exegesis which would discover in the Bible a sanction either for the highly arbitrary arrangements of the Germano-Roman Empire, or for the equally complex English laws which govern the succession to the crown, is as obsolete as the view of Revelation which would look for such information in the pages of Scripture. As soon as the theory of Divine right attempts to justify itself by rational considerations, as soon as it admits that the mode of original appointment and the conditions of continued tenure must be regulated by the varying circumstances of historical development and political expediency, it tends to pass over into one of the other theories—the theory of a social contract or the theory of utility. And as a matter of fact the

theory of Divine right has seldom been maintained in a pure and unadulterated form.

2. I come then, secondly, to the social contract theory. This is the view which is found either as a substitute for, or side by side with, the theory of Divine right in the pages of some Christian Fathers. *Generale quippe pactum est societatis humanae obtemperare regibus suis,* says St. Augustine. Towards the end of the eleventh century (as has recently been pointed out by Mr. Carlyle in the pages of *The Economic Review*[1]), this idea definitely supplanted the earlier theory of Divine right. It takes its place in the Decretum of the Canonist Gratian as the recognised ecclesiastical theory about the basis of political obligation—a position which it retains throughout the medieval period, except (1) in the Ghibelline apologists of Imperial Divine right, and (2) in so far as it was superseded by the adoption of the Aristotelian view in the writings of Thomas Aquinas and his followers. The theory of the social contract is of course best known in the form or forms which it assumes in the Seventeenth and early Eighteenth Centuries. Most of you no doubt know something of the famous system of Hobbes. Mankind was originally (it tells us) a mass of independent units, in a state of perpetual war of every man with every man. In such a state of things there were no duties, and therefore practically no rights, since every man had an equal right to do or to take anything which he chose to think necessary to his own conservation. How in this state of things infants, not yet in a position to contract with their parents, managed nevertheless to get born and nourished and educated up to manhood does not distinctly appear. But gradual experience of the evils of this state of things at length culminated in a mass meeting of primitive men, at which they agreed to lay down their natural liberty of doing what they liked, and covenanted to obey a sovereign, i.e. that man or

[1] Cf. *Economic Review,* July and October 1895.

assembly of men whom the majority should choose. Observe that Hobbes is deeply conscious of the necessity for some rational justification for the despotism of a bare majority—the system which seems so obvious to the popular democratic mind of modern times. The original agreement to pass out of the state of nature and elect a ruler must, according to Hobbes, be absolutely unanimous: no one can be deprived of his natural rights save by his own consent. If he dissents, however, he remains in a state of nature outside the political society, and may therefore be lawfully killed by those who are within it. Once in the society he is bound by the vote of the majority in the choice of a ruler, just because he had himself agreed to be so bound. Once appointed, the ruler and all his successors must be absolute. Sovereign power can neither be divided nor limited. Hobbes's practical object was of course to supply a rational justification for absolute monarchy. To make the social contract theory available for this purpose, he had to saddle it with many arbitrary and inconsistent additions. It was assumed that the contract must always in actual fact take the form which happened to commend itself to the political views of Thomas Hobbes. In Locke the theory, stripped of these arbitrary restrictions, becomes the theoretical basis of English Whiggism. In Locke the power entrusted to the ruler is a limited authority, and must be used for the purposes for which it is given. The ruler who abuses it may lawfully be deposed by the subject. In Rousseau the social contract theory undergoes a further transformation in the interests of revolutionary democracy. Here once again the necessity is felt for the justification of majority-rule: the general rule to which the individual submits himself is (according to Rousseau, or at least to Rousseau at some moments) the absolutely unanimous will of all. And this will, though it binds, binds not always. The general will may change, and consequently no government is lawful under which the people are not assembled at frequent intervals and asked whether they still approve of the continuance of the existing constitution and of the continued tenure of office by its existing *personnel*. How on these principles we could justify even the detention of an offender for a single hour without the previous assembling of the whole nation to ascertain whether perchance the general will may not have changed since the law was passed, is a question not easily answered.

I will not attempt to examine in detail the difficulties involved in the various forms of the contract theory. Following the transformations which it undergoes as it passes from Hobbes to Locke, and from Locke to Rousseau, one feels that the idea of an actual historical contract tends to pass more and more out of sight. Rousseau at all events does not believe in the mass meeting of primitive men (survivals of whom he is inclined to see in the pongo and the orang-outang); and, as he very reasonably disputes the right of primitive man to bind his posterity for all time, the question of the historical contract now becomes of no practical importance. Criticism upon the theory from the historical point of view would therefore be superfluous. Nor would Rousseau himself have pretended that in recent times—even in the most advanced political societies of his day, in his native Geneva for instance—any such constitution as he contemplates ever had been voted into being by such a universal suffrage as his theory postulates. The *Contrat Social* is rather a speculation as to what an ideal political society should be than a theory as to our duty towards existing constitutions. In order to subject the theory to any profitable discussion, we must disengage it from what we may call its historical accidents, and get to the real principle involved in every actual or possible theory of social contract. And the idea which lies at the bottom of the social contract view is the idea of government by consent. The individual is supposed to be born with a mass of rights and liberties which he can only be contracted out of by his own consent. A general liberty to do and say what he likes is assumed to be the normal and natural condition of human nature. All restraint or coercion from without is assumed to be an invasion of this natural liberty, and to require artificial justification—justification which, at least except in so far as it can be shown to be absolutely necessitated by the rights of others, can only arise from the individual's free consent.

At the present day the theory of an actual historical contract, supposed to have taken place at some assignable moment in the past, has indeed been finally dissipated by our improved knowledge of primitive history. The fundamental idea of government by consent is, however, very far indeed from being dead and gone. It is hardly possible to open a democratic newspaper or manifesto without coming across reasoning which implies it; while, on the other side, the rights of the individual are asserted in a way which raises the question how, upon such principles, any legislation could be justified of which the individual happens to disapprove. The social contract theory is no longer maintained by philosophers: it would hardly be defended in so many words even by popular writers. But the mode of thought out of which it sprang is as vigorous as ever. If the mind of Mr. Herbert Spencer were as sensitive to the demands of strict logical consistency as that of Hobbes or of Rousseau, it would perhaps have found a place in the " system of Synthetic Philosophy."

Let us then endeavour to fix our attention upon this fundamental part of the social contract theory—the theory of government by consent. Can a man lawfully be coerced without his own consent? If so, why? and how much? The fashionable way of disposing of such questions among superior people is by saying that society is an organism, and that the individual apart from it is a mere abstraction. I do not think this is a mode of treatment which goes to the root of the difficulty. The social organism, in fact, threatens to become as unintelligible a catchword as the rights of man. The idea is true enough in its way, but the phrase is in danger of serving as a mere substitute for thought. Abstraction or not, the individual has certainly got the power, if he likes, of practically isolating himself from the organism to which he owes his being, or of making it the mere instrument of the gratification of his own desires, or of injuring it and doing a good deal towards its actual extinction. By a combination with his fellows he could even conceivably bring the whole mighty organism to an end. If he is to use these his voluntary powers contrary to his own inclination for the conservation of the organism—if, upon occasion, he is to be ready even to sacrifice his own life to its better life—the considerations must be such as will appeal to his reason: and such considerations assuredly are not to be found in the enunciation of a bare scientific platitude about his being part of the social organism, whether the platitude be left in the physiological nakedness of evolutionary science, or be dressed up in all the metaphysical bravery of Hegelian rhetoric. Merely to tell a man that he is part of the social organism supplies him no reason for becoming a martyr or even a decently good citizen.

The objections to the consent view of government may, perhaps, best be stated in the form of a dilemma. Either (a) the consent is made into something so merely virtual and implicit that the worst government in the world could probably lay claim to it or (b) if a real and explicit consent is required, hardly the most democratic government in existence really rests upon any such consent.

Undoubtedly the subject even of Russia or of Turkey consents to the government for fear of worse evils. It is sometimes, indeed, contended that the people are always the real depositaries of ultimate political power. If this means that no government could permanently

rule a nation of which every member was prepared
to submit to death or torture rather than obey it for
a day longer—a mode of deliverance which really
seems to be almost the only remaining hope of such
a people as the unfortunate Armenians—the doctrine
is as true as it is unimportant. But in such cases
people consent to the government merely in the sense
in which a man consents to voluntarily give up his
purse to an armed highwayman. In that sense of the
term every government could claim legitimacy so long
as it is not actually rebelled against. It can supply no
reason against rebellion, as soon as rebellion becomes
possible. If consent is to serve as a criterion of the
legitimacy of a government, it must clearly be a more
explicit consent than this. And it is difficult to see
how such consent can be ascertained by any means
except a vote.

To the ultra-democratic mind it will perhaps be no
difficulty that such a criterion would deprive the Roman
Empire under M. Antoninus, or the British Empire in
India, of all claims to the obedience of its subjects.
With whatever inconsistent reservations on behalf of
extreme necessity or undeveloped peoples or the like,
there are perhaps persons who would be deliberately
prepared to allege that democracy is the only form of
government which can possess a moral claim to
obedience. To such persons it seems a self-evident
law of nature that the minority should submit to the
majority. To make such persons feel the logical
necessity of some justification for this claim on the
part of a possibly ignorant, stupid, or evil-minded
majority would perhaps be an impossible task. They
may possibly with more success be tackled in another
way. Granting the principle of one man one vote to
be not merely an obvious and practically expedient
political arrangement at a certain stage of social
development, but an irrevocable law of nature, we may
ask whether nature has revealed with equal clearness
any particular system of electoral distribution—any

system which shall be entirely beyond the reach of
jerrymandering in the interests of a dominant faction
—whether nature has disclosed with equal self-
evidence to all her chosen oracles the political rights
or no rights of women, and whether the inferiority
of the young man of twenty and three-quarters to his
natural superior of twenty-one and a month is an
equally self-evident deliverance of intuitive reason. I
abstain from raising questions as to the electoral dis-
abilities of lunatics or animals, or from asking how,
in the light of Darwinism, the political equality of the
bushman and the European can be maintained without
bringing into the region of practical politics the en-
franchisement of the ape or the bee. It is enough to
have pointed out that the principle of government by
consent is incapable of being reduced to an exact form.
Its only really logical form is that which would insist
on the actual, formal consent of each individual citizen.
And even so we should have to ask why, supposing the
individual to have consented to the imposition of a law,
he should not be at liberty to withdraw that consent
and ask for its repeal the moment that he finds himself
in the hands of the police.

It will be urged perhaps, " But surely a man is
bound to keep his own promises." Why so? What
moral obligation can there be on the part of the natural
man in the Hobbian state of nature? If you invest
the natural man with duties, why stop at the duty of
keeping contracts? And if he is bound to any duties,
surely a duty of contributing to social good is as
obvious as the duty of keeping promises. And if a
man is bound to contribute to social good, whether he
has promised to do so or not, no contract is required
to justify such interference with him as will actually
conduce to social good. If and in so far as government interference does not contribute to social good,
no contract will give it a right to command or create
a moral obligation to obey. In short, once recognise
a man's moral obligations towards his fellows, and all

the paraphernalia of the contract become superfluous and unmeaning.

3. Thus we are brought to the last and (as it seems to me) the only tenable view as to the basis of political obligation—the view which finds it in the end which government serves. Argument is scarcely needed to prove this view when once it is clearly stated. If man has no end or τέλος or highest good, if there is nothing which it is right or reasonable that he should be rather than anything else, if there is no one kind of life which a man *ought* to lead in preference to any other kind, then no possible machinery of original contract in the past or of counting heads in the present can possibly create a moral obligation to obey the State or to do or abstain from doing anything which pleases us. If, however, there is an end which man is meant to serve, something which he ought to be, a kind of life which he ought to lead, then surely no further justification can be wanted for compelling him to lead that sort of life and to make it possible for other people. The fact that he does not like that sort of life is no justification for his not leading it—no reason why he should not be made to lead it by every kind of force or coercion which will actually have the effect of assisting him to do so. There can be no injustice in any kind or sort of interference which will insure a man attaining the true end of his being. If the end is the intrinsically right and reasonable end, we need ask for no further reason why it should be pursued.

I have ventured provisionally to call this view the utilitarian theory of political obligation. Up to this point we may claim for that theory something like general acceptance among serious thinkers. But here we encounter a most important bifurcation of opinion. By utilitarian I have meant so far merely the view which finds the justification of government in the end which it serves. There remains the all-important question, "What is that end?" As a matter of fact the people called utilitarians have usually maintained

31

that the end is pleasure. How on such a view of human nature a basis can be found for any sort of moral or any sort of political obligation, is a question which I must not stop to ask. Why, if the end of life be simply pleasure, the individual should ever trouble his head about anybody's pleasure but his own, is too large a question to enter upon here. But so far the utilitarians are undoubtedly logical and consistent in maintaining that, if pleasure is the end of the individual, it must also be the end of the State. The exercise of State authority would then be justified exactly in so far as it tends to swell the sum of human pleasure. Such is the hedonistic-utilitarian view. It is a view which I reject, but which I have no time to discuss further.

On the other hand, we have the Aristotelian theory which, agreeing with the utilitarian in basing the authority of the State upon its tendency to promote human well-being, differs from it profoundly in its view as to what human good really is. Aristotle makes εὐδαιμονία, or well-being, the ultimate end of human life; but by εὐδαιμονία he does not mean pleasure. Even happiness is a very ambiguous and unsatisfactory translation of the word. Pleasure is undoubtedly a part of human well-being. I know this is denied by some of our superfine thinkers. Yet ask them the simple question—" Of two kinds of food equally wholesome, and equally cheap and easy of acquisition, would not every rational man prefer that which gives him most pleasure, supposing the said pleasure not to interfere with the attainment of any higher good? Will he not think it rational to prefer the pleasanter both for himself and for others? " I cannot believe that the most idealistic of our friends will answer " No ": and I am quite sure that if he does his practice belies his theory. However, this is an ethical question which I must not pursue further. For myself, with Aristotle and Thomas Aquinas, I look upon pleasure as a part of human good. However much superior other goods may be to pleasure, they would always be better with pleasure than without it. But there are other goods besides pleasure; pleasure is an element in that ideal life which the wise man desires for himself and for others, but it is not the highest or the most important element. Knowledge, or intellectual activity, is a higher element, but not again the highest. And, of all human goods, the highest is goodness or virtue, which for the Christian may be identified with love in its highest and widest sense.

If such is our conception of the end of human life, we must regard it as the end of the State also. I need hardly stay to point out what a profoundly different view of the end and purpose of the State this is to the conception with which we are familiar in ordinary modern politics. And yet a moment's reflection will show how unreasonable and arbitrary it is, upon a non-utilitarian view of human good, to assign any lower function to the State's activity. If man's whole good be pleasure, then undoubtedly the State can only justify interference or excuse non-interference with his life so far as such interference or non-interference will help to attain that end for all its citizens or all mankind. But if man's highest good be something higher than pleasure, on what principle can it be contended that the State must treat him as though he were a mere animal whose sole good is pleasure? And yet such has been the general tendency of our popular political thought. In quite recent times the idea of State interference with morality has, indeed, perhaps become more or less popular. Nobody has ever quite carried the principle of non-interference in matters of morality so far as to insist that a child shall not be taught to speak the truth—and be taught it very dogmatically too—long before it is at all capable of understanding the philosophical basis of the doctrine, still less of doing justice impartially to the reasoning by which that doctrine has been plausibly enough assailed by latitudinarian, casuistical, or sceptical moralists. Yet, the moment

C   33 that religion enters into the question, we have people telling us that that is altogether beyond the province of the State. If religion be regarded as a sort of system of assurance against posthumous risks, there might be something to be said in favour of such a view; though even so, assuming the risks to be real and the security good, I do not quite see why the State should not help its citizens in their other-worldly efforts. To pronounce that the risks are imaginary or the assurance precarious would, of course, be a scandalous violation of the avowed principle of religious neutrality. But, if religion has any effect on man's life here and now, if it is from one point of view a means to good life, from another point of view part of the good life itself, then surely it must be impossible for the State which is a society for the promotion of good life to be indifferent to religion. Only on the supposition that religion has no effect upon life whatever can such indifference be logically justified. And that is a thesis which has very seldom been systematically maintained. Most of those who do not believe that religion is—at least, to some persons and under some circumstances—a help to good life, have held that it is a positive hindrance to it. Such persons are, of course, logically bound to maintain—and in practice they have (to do them justice) very generally acted on that view—that religion is the enemy of the State. Friend or enemy, indifference is equally unjustifiable. And the idea that, while in a general way religion may be deserving of the friendly patronage of the State, one religion is for State purposes as good as another, is likewise a view which will not survive the most superficial examination. For the very conception of good life which is entertained by different religions is not the same. To suppose that the moral ideal of a Mussulman, a Buddhist, and a Christian is the same, is a contention so ignorant and so preposterous that it can only be accounted for by the prevalence of that absurd limitation of view which confines the idea of morality to the observance of a few obvious and for the most part very elementary, external, and negative rules of conduct. Nobody can be at the same time a polygamist and a monogamist—nobody can at one and the same time aim with the Buddhist at extinction, and with the Christian at increased fullness of life. The differences not merely between different religions, but between different sects of the same religion—nay, between schools and shades of thought in the same Church—relate quite as much to ethics as to theology. The moral ideal of a Romanist differs from that of a Protestant; that of the typical High Churchman to some extent from that of the typical Low Churchman; that of the Oxford Movement from that of the progressive High Churchman of the present moment. If the State exists for the preservation of a certain ideal of life, it must surely care that the ideal at which it aims should be a true one. The State cannot therefore be indifferent to the religions which so profoundly affect the ideals of its citizens. The State may, of course, encourage freedom of thought as the best possible means to the discovery of truth and the promotion of religious sincerity. That does not imply indifference. Indifference to questions of religion would imply indifference on questions of morality, and to make the State indifferent on questions of morality would be to give up the great Aristotelian doctrine that the State exists for the promotion of good life.

To consider the applications of this view of the State authority, firstly, to the mutual relations between Church and State; and, secondly, to the relations between the State and individual citizens, will be the object of my next two lectures. Meanwhile, to prevent misunderstanding, let me make two explanations.

1. First, the doctrine does not by itself imply any particular theory as to what should be at any particular time and place the true relations between the State on the one hand, and the Church or the various religious bodies which divide the allegiance of its citizens on

35

the other. Nothing that I have said necessarily implies the existence of an established Church, or rather (to avoid the misleading idea that every Church must be either established or unestablished), what I have said does not imply that any one of the very numerous types of legal relation between the State and the one or more religious societies existing within it is necessarily at all times and in all places the true one. Each and every kind of relation between Church and State may be the right one at a particular time and place; because each and every one of them may be under a particular set of circumstances the most favourable to the good life of its citizens. A State which has no established Church is not necessarily godless: it is not necessarily indifferent to the religion of its subjects or indifferent as to what that religion should be. It may merely hold that, under given circumstances, impartiality on the part of the State as between certain bodies separated by minor differences—with the most fundamental differences impartiality must always be more or less a sham—that with regard to these minor differences the State will best promote the good life of its citizens by entire impartiality and relative non-interference. I say relative non-interference: for absolute non-interference can easily be shown to be an impossibility. The Judicial Committee of the Privy Council has to decide questions of Buddhist ritual as often as questions of Anglican canon law. The Aristotelian theory of the State is not necessarily opposed to any particular view as to the desirable relations between Church and State at a particular time and place. The only argument which it forbids us to use in favour of disestablishment is the plea that the State has got nothing to do with religion. At the same time, I need hardly point out how very largely arguments for disestablishment, arguments against what is called denominational education, and arguments about half a dozen other practical questions of the kind are, as a matter of fact, arguments of the

36

a priori character which ought to have vanished with the professed disappearance from public life of the natural man and all his works.

2. What has been said applies equally to any other kind of interference in matters of morality, of education, of economic organisation. How far State interference actually, under given conditions, will conduce to the growth or just distribution of wealth, to the advancement of knowledge, to the promotion of morality—these are questions which must be decided by experience—actual, specific experience, when we have it, or by prevision based upon our general knowledge of the laws of human nature and human society when specific experience fails us. It is quite consistent to maintain that the State exists to promote morality, but that at the same time it promotes it best by leaving it alone. At the same time, put in this general way, the conclusion would be something of a paradox. The great practical lesson which a true doctrine of the moral basis of State authority teaches us is this—that each question of interference or non-interference must be decided on its own merits. We cannot absolve ourselves from the task of examining the arguments for or against any particular kind of State interference—religious, moral, economic, social —by falling back upon general *a priori* principles either for or against interference or even against interference in any one of the great distinguishable, but of course closely interconnected, departments of human life. We cannot approve or condemn any single measure by simply saying, " This would be interference with religion, or with private morals, or with economics." Of course we may by experience come to certain general conclusions as to the tendency of interference in some particular department. Such experience may lead to some general presumption against certain particular kinds of interference; but still we can never exclude the possibility that, though as a rule interference of a particular kind may be bad,

37

under certain particular circumstances it may be good, or that, though some specific piece of interference is bad, some closely allied piece of interference may be good. We must not, with Mr. Herbert Spencer, assume that, because as a general rule Government departments are worse organised than private firms, therefore the Post Office ought to be given up; or with many Socialists affirm that, because the Post Office is a success, therefore every kind of production could be managed best or could be managed at all by State agency.

Most of the writers who argue for or against State interference, or any particular kind of interference, profess to establish, or at least to confirm, their doctrine by specific experience, but most of them are disposed to fall back on *a priori* theories much wider than are required to support the practical conclusions which have really dictated the theories. In past times the State interfered mistakenly in certain well-known ways with trade and commerce. Hence the theory of orthodox Manchesterian politicians and economists that all State interference with economic organisation is bad. Mr. Herbert Spencer, panic-stricken at the advance of modern Socialism, has been driven to wake the natural man out of his well-earned grave. The Dissenter, holding that the Anglican establishment is a bad thing, feels it necessary to back up his view with a comprehensive doctrine that the State has nothing to do with religion—a theory on which (to its credit be it said) the Nonconformist conscience has always in practice steadily refused to act. J. S. Mill, thinking that the suppression of speculative thought by law or opinion was a bad thing, was driven into the monstrously anti-utilitarian doctrine that neither the State nor society has anything to do with a man's beliefs or private life. As regards belief this view is still popular, while the economic non-intervention theory is of course rapidly disappearing. It has been the object of this lecture to point out that all such limitations of the State's authority are equally inconsistent with the only logically defensible view of the basis of State authority, however strong may be the experiential argument against some particular kinds of interference. The State exists to promote the good life of her citizens: nothing that affects human life can she afford to treat as alien to herself. At the same time, her interest in the highest life of her citizens can as little compel her to any specific kind of interference as a parent can be said to be necessarily indifferent to the highest well-being of his children because at a certain age he declines to enforce their attendance at a particular place of worship or to prescribe the particular way in which they shall spend their pocket-money. We may even push the analogy a little further, and contend that there is an *a priori* probability that the State ought to act on the same principle and an *a priori* presumption against theories which propose that the State shall treat her citizens as mere children, and not rather (if government should still in a sense be paternal) as sons and daughters past the age of school, but economically dependent upon others, are treated by sensible, far-sighted, and affectionate parents. But this is anticipating the subject of my second and third lectures.

III

THE RIGHTS OF THE CHURCH

In my last paper I tried to show that the only tenable view as to the source of the State's authority is that which finds it in the end which the State subserves. Whatever be the true end of human life, the State is a society of men bound together with a view to the promotion of that end. Whatever form of government at a given time and place best promotes that end is the right form of government for that time and place. Any amount of control, interference, coercion, which will really help men to attain to the true end of their being is therefore amply justified. Any interference which does not promote that end lacks moral justification. It may not, of course, always be right to resist any measure which in our opinion does not conduce to the true end of social life, for the consequences of such resistance in weakening respect for law and order are, in the vast majority of cases, far worse than the evil of some particular piece of mistaken or misdirected interference. The very existence of the State depends upon the subordination of private judgement to that of certain constituted authorities. But both the right of the State to command and the right—in case of extreme necessity—of the subject to resist or rebel are founded on the fact that, in Aristotelian phrase, the State exists for the sake of well-being, or —since that is the highest element of well-being—for the sake of virtue.

So far we have only been following the guidance of the first great master of political thought. On two points, however, we are compelled to diverge from Aristotle.

(a) To Aristotle the people whose well-being was to be considered were simply citizens, i.e. a more or less select aristocracy of the whole population, excluding slaves, aliens, and (if possible) most manual labourers. We have to recognise the right of man, as such, to consideration at the hands of the State. This is a point to which I will return hereafter.

(*b*) Agreeing entirely with Aristotle as to the relation between virtue and well-being—agreeing that virtue forms the highest element in this well-being for which the State exists, and the chief condition upon which its other elements depend, we differ from him in our conception of what virtue is. If we are Christians, the ideal life which the State exists to promote must be the Christian life. The differences between the Christian ideal of life and the Aristotelian I must for the present purpose assume to be well known.

To the Christian, then, the State is a society for the promotion of the Christian ideal of life. And how else could we describe the object of the Church? Both Church and State are distinctly societies for promoting the highest kind of life, and if Christianity be true, that kind of life must be the Christian life.

If this be so, we see at once the absolute impossibility of distinguishing the office of the Church from that of the State by dividing life into two mutually exclusive spheres, and assigning one of them to the Church and the other to the State: as, for instance, by saying that the Church has to do with the soul, the State with the body; or that the objects of the Church are spiritual, those of the State temporal; and the like. Such a distinction between the spiritual and the non-spiritual was only possible in ages wherein the spiritual was frankly identified with the posthumous. The object of the Church was simply to help people to go to heaven, while their present happiness—including the moral as distinct from the theological virtues—was wholly made over to the care of the State. It is startling to find such a conception in the *De Monarchia* of Dante. His Ghibellinism caused him to fall behind his great master Thomas Aquinas, though even he makes virtue too exclusively a means to an end outside earthly life. The fact is that each of these societies or organisations, according to the true conception of it, must claim the whole of life as its pro-

41

vince. The State which exists for the sake of good life cannot be indifferent to anything which purports to promote good life. It cannot, therefore, be indifferent to the Christian ideal of life, or even to Christian doctrine. On the other hand, the Church can equally little afford to regard any sphere of life as beyond its province. Even were we prepared to say that the Church exists to promote only the higher of those varied ends of human life which together make up the total well-being or εὐδαιμονία of man, the interconnection of the moral and the material, the spiritual and the carnal, is so close that there is no department of life with which it may not be called to interfere. It might, for instance, be urged that the promotion of comfort and amusement is no part of the end of the Church; but the character of man is so intimately affected by the nature of the comforts and amusements in which he indulges—by having enough comfort and amusement, and not too much, and of the right kind, and so on—that even on this ground it could not be contended in practice that the Church had no concern with such matters. We could not, as a matter of principle, object to the Church, even in its corporate capacity, conducting model theatres or reformed public-houses, however strongly we might feel the practical inexpediency of such enterprises. But though in practice we should no doubt only justify interference with such matters on the part of the Church where a direct moral end is to be attained thereby and the work cannot otherwise be done, I do not think it is necessary, as a matter of pure theory, even to limit the sphere of the Church to this—in the stricter sense—moral side of things. Whatever is really part of good life, as a Christian understands it, is part of the end of the Church. The Church has always recognised the collection and distribution of alms as one of its most prominent functions; and it is arbitrary to say that its concern for material well-being must stop at the bare necessaries of life. It

42

has always been recognised in theory that education is part of its work, and it is a poor conception of education which supposes that it must stop at fifteen or at twenty-five. With whatever forms no part of good life Christians can have nothing to do, whether *qua* Christian, or *qua* Churchman, or *qua* citizen, or *qua* anything else.

It may be well, perhaps, to illustrate a little more in detail the impossibility of reconciling the conflicting claims of Church and State by confining each of them to some one sphere or department of life. The most obvious point of contact is, of course, the possession and use of property. Practically in modern times the Church cannot effectively carry on its work without property. Wherever there is property, questions must constantly arise as to its ownership, its uses, and its obligations, with which, even on the most minimising view of its functions, the State must necessarily concern itself. Even apart from property, membership of a voluntary society carries with it both duties and rights which the State may at any time be called upon to enforce or to protect. Even, therefore, in the exercise of its most indefeasible power of expelling its own members, the Church necessarily touches the rights and the reputation of citizens, which it is the inevitable duty of the State to protect; just as it does the rights of a man who has joined a club or a joint-stock company. I am not, of course, saying that in practice it is not possible to reduce to a minimum the risk of direct collision between Church and State, even with a State that is in no sense Christian. I am only contending that it is impossible to mark off any sphere of life as belonging wholly to one or the other, or to regard the two bodies as societies whose respective functions go on without either interference or coincidence. Dealing with the same subject-matter, they inevitably come into constant contact, and the nature of that contact must necessarily be determined by the extent to which both are actuated by the same aims, principles, and ideals.

43

If, then, Church and State are two societies which
exist for the same purpose, why should their separate
existence be maintained? Why should they not fuse?
I need hardly point out that, even where they are composed of the same persons, it does not necessarily
follow that the societies themselves must be identical.
The same body of persons may be organised in two
totally different ways for two different purposes, or
even for different contributions to the same ultimate
end, and may therefore form quite distinct societies.
The same individuals may form at the same time an
army and a Commonwealth, and the government and
organisation of the two bodies may be dissimilar. But
where the societies exist for the same purpose, the
maintenance of two distinct societies would naturally
seem to require some justification. *Prima facie,* the
conclusion to which our reasoning might so far seem
to point would be that the Church ought to be swallowed up in the State. This is, of course, the tendency
of the view which is commonly described as Erastian.
It is, of course, substantially the view of the ideal
relation between Church and State adopted by Dr.
Arnold. And if to some such a view should seem
inconsistent with a divine constitution once for all imposed by Christ upon His Church, we still do not
escape the difficulty. For if the Church cannot be
swallowed up in the State, at least on the strictest
ecclesiastical principles there is no reason why the
State should not be swallowed up into the Church. Does
not, it may be said, the Papal State of thirty years ago
(however unsatisfactory in practice) represent the
ideal relation between Church and State in a truly
Christian country? Some of the critics of the Christian Social Union seem really to be a little afraid lest
we should be tending towards such a state of things in
this country; and there may, therefore, be a practical
as well as a theoretical advantage in asking ourselves
definitely why we reject either the Arnoldian or the
Papal State view of the relation between the Church

44

and State, while refusing firmly to recognise any fundamental or theoretical difference between their spheres or ends.

I. It is clearly only in the case of the Christian State that such a relation becomes possible. That Church and the State should be two societies composed of exactly the same persons is certainly the ideal at which we ought to aim. But we need hardly point out that it is only an ideal. Arnold was, indeed, prepared to exclude Jews and Atheists from all political rights, on the ground that they did not and could not share the ideal which the Christian State proposed to itself. I need hardly point out the practical objections and inconveniences of this system, or insist on the fact that the disfranchisement of a few hundred thousand Jews and avowed Atheists would still leave our own or any other State very far removed indeed from the ideal of a Christian society. But the exclusion from the ecclesiastical society of some persons who are included in the civil society does not necessarily prevent the State being in a real sense Christian. It does not prevent the Christian using his political power for the ends which Christianity teaches him to be the true ends of all human society; and in so far as Christians are in a majority in the State, in so far as the conscience of the community is Christian, its legislation and policy, foreign and domestic, will actually be directed towards the accomplishment of such ends. The State may be Christian though it includes a minority of non-Christians, just as it may be English while including thousands of citizens of French or German blood. Of course the existence of non-Christians in the State does often profoundly affect the means which the Christian statesman will employ to realise his Christian ends. To enforce Christian education on the Jewish child would not, of course, really tend to promote the spiritual well-being of the community. Christianity enforced at the point of the bayonet may sometimes, indeed, become sincerely orthodox in the

45

second or third generation, but the Christian spirit is apt to evaporate in the process. On the other hand, it is well to point out that we do, and rightly do, on certain points enforce the Christian ideal of life upon persons who do not share it; e.g. we suppress Juggernaut processions and suttee in India, and suicide, abortion, and other pagan practices in England. The existence of non-Christians in the community is quite consistent with the State being in a real sense Christian; but it is a fatal objection to the actual fusion of Church and State. The disfranchisement of Atheists and Jews would not tend to the $\epsilon\dot{v}\delta\alpha\iota\mu\text{ov}\acute{\iota}\alpha$ of a modern community, even where their ideals really differ from those of the Christians, while 'the exclusion from political rights of all who failed to come up to some standard of Christian life which the Church might be quite right in imposing upon its own members would be fatal to the very existence of the State. Such a State would, in Aristotelian phrase, be full of enemies. And then in practice we are happily able to recognise that many persons of non-Christian belief do share the Christian ideal of life at least quite sufficiently for practical co-operation in political and social effort. Even with persons whose ideal of life falls grievously short of the Christian standard, it is well that we should co-operate with them up to whatever point they are prepared to follow us. The State is much more than a society for the promotion of order and sanitation, but there is no reason why we should not, both in political and other ways, co-operate for the promotion of order and sanitation with people who can see no end in human life but pleasure, and who tend practically towards identifying pleasure with mere animal satisfaction.

2. Even where the two societies are actually composed of the same persons, practical convenience may render a differentiation of function between its different organs extremely desirable. The ideal magistrate exists for the promotion of spiritual life quite as much

as the ideal priest. And, in so far as each approaches the true ideal of human nature, he might with less inconvenience undertake the functions of the other, though it is possible that a certain adaptation of character to function may be regarded as itself a part of this true ideal. But, whatever we may think of the ideal magistrate and the ideal clergyman, I need hardly insist on the fact that many relatively good judges would make very bad bishops, and many good bishops would make bad judges. This much even Arnold would probably have admitted, though he does suggest the desirability of ecclesiastical duties being under exceptional circumstances undertaken by civil and military officers. But this consideration will carry us further. Not merely may it be desirable that the officials in the two communities should be different, but the whole organisation that serves best for carrying on one set of social activities may be wholly unsuited to another set of activities, though both of them may have precisely the same objects. The functions of Parliament are quite as sacred as those of any ecclesiastical authority whatever. And yet a Parliament, though composed entirely of Churchmen, might be an even less satisfactory organ than our present Convocation for the expression of the highest mind of the nation on such matters as the choice of a hymn-book, the amendment of the Prayer-book, or the appointment to ecclesiastical offices. For practical purposes, therefore, the separate organisation of Church and State, even in the midst of the closest harmony and alliance, may still, though, for all that we have so far seen, it *need* not on any ground of principle, be desirable.

What I have already said implies that, though Church and State aim at the same ultimate ends, there is still in a sense a difference of function between them. What is that difference? That brings me to my third point.

3. There is one essential difference between Church and State which is ignored by thinkers of the Arnold

47

School. There is no difference of sphere between Church and State, but there is a fundamental difference of method. It is of the essence of the State to be compulsive. It is of the essence of the Church to be a voluntary society. Membership of the Church is based upon a voluntary allegiance to a certain ideal of life, intellectual acceptance of a certain view of the relation between God and man, and devotion to an historical Person in whom that true relation has, according to the Christian idea, found its supreme manifestation. Great varieties of intellectual interpretation may be quite compatible with joint membership of the society; devotion to a moral ideal may be a bond of union incomparably more important than intellectual agreement, but some measure of intellectual agreement is necessarily implied in the mere acceptance of the ideal. Hence from its very nature the Christian society is ideally one which the individual must be free to join, and free to leave, and from which he is capable of being expelled. Hence an absolute impossibility of complete fusion with a society whose essential attributes are compulsion and all-inclusiveness.

And now I will venture to suggest a few possible applications of the doctrine I have been attempting to defend. I do not mean to discuss any of these questions in detail; but I should like just to notice a few of the practical problems on which a clear grasp of theoretical principles may possibly throw some light.

(1) There is the question of the permanent constitutional relations between Church and State. To ask whether this or that piece of State interference is or is not overstepping the limits of State authority, or encroaching upon the province of the Church, is, upon the view which I have been attempting to maintain, a question to which no definite answer can be given. No department of human life can be regarded as wholly beyond the scope of the State's interest, if the State is to deal with life as a whole; and if in so doing its views and policy diverge from those of the Church,

collision is inevitable The only way of settling whether this or that piece of State interference ought to be attempted by the State or to be submitted to by the Church, is to ask whether, under given circumstances, such interference will conduce to the end which Church and State alike have in view. It is impossible, for instance, to deny that the appointment of bishops in the Greek Church by the Sultan, or even in our own Church by the Prime Minister, is a most distinct invasion of the Church's position as a free, voluntary, autonomous religious society. Equally impossible is it to deny that the appointment of persons who exercise such an influence over the social and moral life of the country is a matter which vitally affects the State, even apart from any civil privileges or responsibilities with which the State may see fit to invest such Church officials. The practical question for the Church to consider is whether, under given circumstances, submission to such State appointment will do more to enable the Church to realise her true end than resistance to it. It can never be right to disturb an existing arrangement of that kind, any more than to attempt any other change of constitutional machinery, on mere abstract *a priori* grounds. It can never be wrong to resist where resistance will really tend to the common good. Church and State, or more frequently certain authorities in Church and State, may take different views as to the interests of Church and State; but real collision between the true interests of Church and State is as impossible as a want of coincidence between the convex and the concave sides of the same curve. I have said nothing as to the question whether the existing arrangement does not on the whole express the real mind even of the Church better than any other practicable arrangement, since that is a question which does not naturally arise out of our argument.

(2) Let us consider the application of our principle to such a matter as religious education. To assign

secular education to the State and religious education to the Church implies precisely that division of life into water-tight compartments against which I want, above all things, to protest. What a naïve idea it is to suppose that a few hours' biblical instruction can override the influence of six times as many hours devoted to an education which is avowedly non-religious, and may be actually anti-religious in its tone, temper, or personal influences! Those who want to get admission for the clergy for an hour a week into schools, primary or secondary, at the cost of abandoning all the rest of the children's time to an education which avowedly regards the religious side of life as a sort of taboo, about which nothing can be said, had better ask themselves what influence the weekly theological lessons, regularly given by well-educated priests in every lycée in France, have produced upon the religion of the educated male laity in that country, or the regular religious lessons of Protestant pastors in Germany upon the religious and moral ideas of German artisans. Does anyone seriously suppose that it is not possible to teach Voltairism or Bradlaughism as effectually in a history lesson as in a Bible lesson? or that it will be possible to lay down rules for the exclusion of such teaching which could not be evaded, except at the cost of taking all the individuality, and therefore all the heart and all the life, out of all the teacher's lessons? On the other hand, it is unreasonable to resent the teaching of religion under School Board authority by School Board teachers as a violation of the theoretical rights of the Church. An ideal Church would, no doubt, be fit to be entrusted not only with the religious but with the whole education of the people, and no department of education can possibly lie beyond the province of the Church. The real question is, Under given circumstances, what is the best practical arrangement for securing the maximum moral and intellectual progress of the people? It is important to recognise that an education that is given by Churchmen, that is strongly dogmatic and unimpeachably orthodox, may not only be intellectually bad and inefficient, but may be profoundly unchristian. There may be and are Bible lessons which contain no religion; while a schoolmaster who loses his temper or neglects his duty will give more unchristian teaching than all his Bible lessons will ever undo; while an education that is not even given by Christians may be to a very large extent, though it must of course be imperfectly, Christian in its tone and tendency. The practical question is, How can we get the maximum of Christian education under given circumstances? Do not let us mistake clerical predominance for Christianity, nor its exclusion for educational efficiency. Respect for the rights of the parental conscience is up to a certain point, as a means to an end, conducive to the true end of the State; but the real interests of education, i.e. of the State itself, must not be sacrificed either to theoretical claims of the State or to theoretical principles of religious equality. It we push the parental conscience argument far enough, the State would be bound to provide a separate teacher for the children of any parent who was too stupid to be able to find any other parent who shared his conscientious convictions upon theology, or history, or astronomy.

(3) A variety of questions are coming to the front as to the comparative merits of voluntary association and of State interference in such matters as hospital management, the relief of the poor, the care of orphans, etc. Here we are not met by a formal rivalry between the State and the Church in her corporate capacity. But practically many voluntary philanthropic agencies owe the larger part of their funds, their workers, and their inspiration to the activity of the various religious societies within the State. Here again I would insist that we should confine attention to the real question at issue, instead of losing ourselves in aimless abstract discussions as to the respective

provinces of State and Church or of State and voluntary effort. It is impossible for the Church to deny that the encouragement and the organisation of charity are part of her work without proving unfaithful to her whole past history. As with charity, so with education; the Church was at work before it ever occurred to the State to occupy itself with the matter. If and when the time should come when any particular department of charitable work can be better done by the State than by the Church, the Church should not complain of being robbed of her heritage, but should simply rejoice at having done her work so well. The Church never does her work better than when it stimulates the State into doing its duty, whether that end is accomplished by the thunders of a Hildebrand or by the agitations of the modern press and pulpit. For be it remembered, the undertaking of such tasks by the State by no means implies their abandonment by the Church. We have pretty well discovered by this time that the success or failure of State interference depends mainly upon the way in which it is administered; and the way in which such matters as the Poor Law are worked in a given district depends very largely upon the success of the Church in her most characteristic task of inspiring with the love of God and man the men and women who are to do the work. Particularly is this the case where the State has to work by voluntary and unpaid agency. There are some valuable remarks in this sense in a recent article of Canon Barnett's in the *Contemporary Review,* and in many other writings of his. He pleads for the recognition of work upon Town Councils, Boards of Guardians, Charity Organisation Committees and the like, as definite spheres of Christian work, and for the extension of State control to hospitals and the care of the poor at the expense of voluntary organisations. In principle I entirely sympathise with his remarks. On the other hand, I am not sure that he allows sufficiently for the greater enthusiasm, elasticity, and variety which may sometimes be secured by voluntary agency. It is hardly conceivable, for instance, that such a man as Dr. Barnardo could have done the work which he has done under the control of a government emigration office; or that the most exemplary Board of Guardians could carry on a Labour Shelter with the success which has attended the Church Army. All government action must follow general rules; the essence of successful philanthropy is to be particular, and, I will add, very often to be much more despotic than a democratically controlled government office can dare to be. All I want to plead for here is the discussion of such questions upon their merits, apart alike from the ecclesiastical prejudice against the supposed unholiness of the State and all its doings, and the political bias against every undertaking that can be stamped with the damning epithet " denominational." I may perhaps add a word, by the way, on the fallacy often committed in discussions upon Socialism, i.e. the fallacy of assuming that the question at issue is always one of State action *versus* Individualism. *Laissez-faire* in its fullest extent is doomed, whether in economics or in anything else. The question of the future is really between State action and various forms of voluntary co-operation. And, however far State action may be pushed in the future, its success will largely depend upon the State's activities being worked in a spirit which it will always want voluntary co-operation to generate and to keep alive, and especially that highest form of voluntary co-operation which we call the Church.

(4) And, lastly, I come to a question which especially concerns us as members of the Christian Social Union. This is the question of the interference of the Church and the clergy in political and economic struggles. If the view which I have been taking of the Church's mission be a true one, no sphere of life can possibly be placed beyond the province of an ideal clergy's guiding

and inspiring influence. The primary mission of the clergy is to teach men their duty, and to make them do it. And there is no department of duty more important, and none in which men need help and guidance more, than in those which relate to voting at elections or in public bodies, or to questions of selling our own labour and buying that of our fellow-men. To exclude the Church from a voice in such matters is to exclude her from all share in the practical life of the nation; it is to say that the man who is set up in a pulpit to teach people their duty is to confine himself to doctrines which have no immediate practical effect upon the life of men, or to ethical platitudes which shall be in no danger of disturbing the complacent and respectable religious sinner, or of attracting those to whom the gospel has long been presented in the light of a worn-out fable. All that is moral lies within the province of the Church, and therefore of its official organs; and morality covers the whole of life. On the other hand, when we come to the practical question whether an interference or a manifesto, rhetoric or partisanship, of a particular kind, under particular circumstances, is or is not conducive to that good life which it is the Church's mission to promote—that is a question about which it is always possible to say a good deal on both sides. But remember that the question is always one of expediency, not of principle. All sorts of considerations may rightly induce a clergyman to be silent, in the pulpit or out of it, even upon matters about which he personally may have strong convictions. Where *party* politics are concerned, it is nearly always best—as it seems to me—in the pulpit to confine ourselves to principles which, however strongly they may seem to us to point one way in the immediate political struggle of the moment, may still conceivably be interpreted as pointing in other directions by conscientious Christian men. On other matters, such as disputed economic or social questions, a thousand considerations may dictate silence—a consciousness of our own incapacity to judge, or at least to dictate, the evil of dividing congregations, the desirability of keeping alive a sense of personal responsibility, the general evils of excessive clerical meddling, and the desirability of avoiding the ill-feeling which it creates. Such considerations might be multiplied indefinitely, and balanced by no less numerous considerations on the other side. All that I am claiming now is that such questions should be discussed upon their true grounds, not upon the basis of any narrow *a priori* theory as to the proper province of the Church or of the clergyman. And such questions are not confined to mere utterance. It was not by mere talking that the Church owed its original conquest over the Roman empire. Every voluntary society, from a Church to a West End club, must have some discipline. Theoretically, we must assert the Church's right to exercise discipline as much in the present day as in the days of the Fathers or the Schoolmen. Practically, we shall most of us admit that in the vast majority of cases the only form of discipline which is likely to be effective at the present day is an action on public opinion. And in the pursuit of its true end the Church has the right to use any and every means of action upon public opinion that is likely to be effective. Churchmen have, for instance, just as much right to combine to choose their tradesmen in such a way as will best secure the Church's end of universal well-being, as a dining-club has to choose them with a view to the attainment of its own peculiar end, e.g. the maximum of gastronomic enjoyment with the minimum of expenditure. If sweating and long hours, no chairs and bad sanitary arrangements, are inconsistent with general well-being, there cannot possibly be a task more proper to the Church's function than the boycotting of tradesmen who offend in these ways by every means which the law allows. Wherever the State puts down such things effectively, there, of course, the interference of the Church is superfluous. But all through her history the Church has been effective, and has fulfilled her mission, just in proportion as she has undertaken all such tasks needed for the general well-being as were actually neglected by the State. There are functions of teaching and worship which can never be surrendered to the State, just because from their very nature they belong essentially to the voluntary associations of believers in Christ; but to restrict the Church's work to these is to lose sight of the fact that even these things are but means to an end, and that the true end of all the Church's work is not worship or belief, but the promotion of a certain kind of life. Life in Christ means treating one another as brethren; neglect of anything that concerns our brethren's well-being must, therefore, be impossible to a society of men pledged to live, and to help one another in living, the life that Christ would have them lead.

I have so far studiously avoided all directly theological discussion. I have assumed, as I am entitled to assume in this society, that we all agree that there is, and always will be, such an institution as the Church of Christ. I have purposely avoided all those questions as to its nature and constitution which divide Christians, and even members of our own branch of Christ's Church. But perhaps the course of the discussion may have suggested that some of these controversies might with advantage be transferred to another plane of thought than that upon which they are often argued. I have tried to exhibit the function of the Church as being the promotion of the true and highest well-being of the human race. If that was what Christ lived and died for, that must surely be the purpose for which His Church was founded. From the State it is marked off mainly by its being a voluntary society, and a society necessarily confined to those who are in some sense of the word Christians, however widely it may be possible and expedient to extend that term. From all other voluntary societies it is marked off as the society which ought ideally to be all-embracing, to include within and subordinate to itself all other voluntary societies among Christian men. Now, would it not be better if questions relating to the organisation, the discipline, the unity, of the Church were more often discussed on this basis—by asking what kind of organisation, of discipline, of unity, is most conducive to the end for which the Church exists? Of course I do not mean that precedent, history, tradition, authority are to go for nothing; the maintenance of historic continuity is itself an important means to the fulfilment of the Church's true end. But would it not be better if the question whether the true Church be visible or invisible, whether its unity should be outward and visible or invisible and spiritual, what degree of uniformity in organisation is required to constitute unity and so on—would it not be better if these questions were sometimes discussed on the basis which I have suggested? If that were done, it could hardly be maintained that disunion and absence of organisation could be otherwise than hindrances to the Church's efficiency in doing its proper work, except among those who think that the work of the Church is and should be limited to preaching, worship, and the saving of individual souls. Competition between soul-saving organisations might in itself be a good thing; it can hardly be a good thing in a society which has for its object the regulation and co-ordination of all the voluntary efforts and spiritual forces of a community with a view to the production of the highest life. Still less could anyone think that invisibility could conduce to this effective action of the Church upon a nation's life. Is there anything that the enemies of the Church and of her good life would wish more than that she should be invisible? Nothing but the Church's failure to attain, or even it may be to aim, at her true end, could ever make outward division a good thing, even as the less of two evils. But while we shall perhaps plead for unity of organisation as a part of the true ideal of the Christian Church more effectively when we argue for it as a means to enable the Church to do her proper work than when we attempt to base it merely upon a particular exegesis of isolated texts, the conception of unity to which we shall be led by such considerations will not compel us to ignore that measure of unity and organised co-operation which is still possible even in the midst of formal schism. Let us urge that the highest unity does include, though it is not chiefly constituted by, unity of organisation; but let us not forget that, the more we can exhibit the spectacle of union among Christians and Christian bodies in an organised campaign against sin and misery and social evils of every kind, the more we shall be enabling people to rise to some faint imagination of what an ideal, all-embracing, undivided Church of Christ would really be. The best way to bring about the union that ought to be is surely by making the very most of such union as is or might be among Christian people and Christian societies.

IV

THE RIGHTS OF THE INDIVIDUAL

In my first paper an attempt was made to show that the only tenable view as to the source of State authority was the view which finds it in the tendency of the State to enable a man to realise the true end of his being, to be the best and highest that he has it in him to be, to lead the best sort of life which he has it in him to lead. And from this view of the source of State authority we inferred a doctrine as to its limits, viz. that any sort of State interference is justified which really does help men to lead such lives: no interference is justified which does not conduce towards this end. In the present paper I propose to look at the matter from the side of the individual and to ask what effect this doctrine has upon the individual and his rights.

We have held that whatever in the way of State action tends to the general good is justified; whatever militates against it is not justified. Hence we may say that the only rights which the State can be called upon to recognise in the individual are such " liberties of action and acquisition " as tend to the general good. Usually, of course, the term " rights " is confined to liberties which can be enforced by law. Legal rights are, of course, such liberties of action and acquisition as are actually secured to the individual by the positive law of a particular State. In the language of moral and political philosophy, we generally mean by rights such liberties as *ought* to be secured by law, though in a looser sense we may apply the term to liberties which society ought to respect, though without implying that they ought necessarily to be legally enforced. We say that we have a right to courteous treatment, or to be told the truth, or the like, without implying that discourtesy or lying ought to be actionable. Such a doctrine may, at first sight, appear to hand over the individual, bound hand and foot, to the tender mercies of the modern Leviathan. It may seem to make the State everything and the individual nothing. " Has the individual no moral right even against the State or against society itself? " it may be asked. That is the question which I want to discuss in the present paper.

There are, I think, two senses in which it may be said that the individual has rights against the State, though—as I hope to show—neither of these admissions implies that the individual, under any circumstances whatever, has a right to do what is really contrary to the general good.

1. I have already explained that by the general good I do not mean the general pleasure. There are many things which might increase the general sum of human pleasure which would nevertheless not tend to the improvement of human character or of true well-being. These things the State can have no right to do. The extinction of the unfit, whether young or old, by summary execution, might no doubt solve many social problems, and I cannot doubt that (if it could really be carried out) it would increase the sum of pleasure measured merely quantitatively—at least it would do so if man were really nothing but a pleasure-seeking animal. But if we believe that for society to adopt this rough-and-ready way out of its difficulties, for the individual parent to rid himself of superfluous children by infanticide, and for the State to allow him to do so, would not really be to the highest good of either individual or society, then, of course, this admission does not really constitute an exception to the doctrine that all rights have their origin in the general good. Still, if there are some things which the State is morally not at liberty to do for its own convenience, we may so far hold that the individual has certain rights even against the State—the right, for instance, to life. At the same time, of course, everyone admits that there are some occasions when the real and highest interest of the State demands that the right shall be no longer recognised, and then it ceases to be a right. The right is, after all, conditioned by considerations of true public well-being, though—once again—public well-

being includes moral and intellectual well-being, and not merely pleasure.

2. There is a more real sense in which we may admit that the individual has rights against the State. We have so far talked vaguely about general good or social well-being. It is now time to remind ourselves that there is no such thing as public or general or State well-being that is not ultimately the well-being of a certain definite number of individual persons. To say that we should aim at the greatest happiness or the greatest good gives us no sufficient guidance. If we suppose that we have a lot of happiness or good to distribute, and that we can really distribute it among a definite number of persons like so much cake, it is clear that we could produce the same total amount of happiness by distributing it evenly among the persons or by giving it all to one. The total amount of good is the same whether I make ten persons slightly happy or one person just ten times as happy. Nor does the addition of the Benthamite formula " of the greatest number " supply us with a satisfactory principle of distribution, for on that principle I might divide it all among six out of the ten, and give none at all to the remaining four. We are then brought face to face with the great question, " On what principle ought we to distribute well-being, in so far as it lies in our power, whether by State action or by private conduct, to effect its distribution? "

The rational and self-evident principle seems to me to be contained in the maxim, " Everyone to count for one, and nobody for more than one."

" What! " I think I hear my Individualist friend exclaiming, " the drivelling drunkard to be treated as well as the sober, respectable virtuous citizen! " Such an objection—which I hear formed the substance of a sermon recently delivered in an Oxford College Chapel with the view of counteracting the influence of the Christian Social Union—such an objection really shows a curious inability to grasp an abstract principle.

61

The supposed consequence by no means follows, for—

(1) Such an arrangement would not really be for the good of the drunkard. The kindest thing you could do to him would be to starve or lash him into working and keeping sober.

(2) The drunkard is a public nuisance, and if we actually in practice assigned him, without labour, remuneration equal to that of a deserving and hard-working man, we should be violating the equal rights of the scores of hard-working men who would suffer from the encouragement to idleness afforded by such a principle of distribution. To place the idle drunkard in concrete fact on an equality with the sober worker would not be treating him as of exactly equal importance to any one other man, but treating him as though he were of as much importance as twenty, fifty, or a hundred other men. Equality of consideration is not the same thing as equality of distribution.

(3) Nothing hinders our even saying that merit ought to be rewarded. This raises a difficult speculative question which I do not propose to enter upon now. I will only point out that our maxim merely implies that all men are to be dealt with on equal principles. A is not to claim from society what is not conceded to B simply because A is A and B is B. If A is a better man than B, well and good. Let him be rewarded, if you like, provided that under the same circumstances you are prepared to offer a similar reward to B.[1]

I have already, in the pages of *The Economic Review*,[2] endeavoured to explain and to defend this

---

[1] Personally, I should be disposed to deny the right to reward if that means "the better a man becomes, the more material wealth he should enjoy." The true reward of superior excellence (moral or intellectual) would seem to be the opportunity for exercising it together with that amount of "external supply" (as Aristotle would put it) which is most favourable to its unimpeded and therefore enjoyable exercise. It is reasonable that the good man should be happy, but he should get his superior happiness out of the exercise of his faculties under the most favourable conditions.

[2] "What is Justice?" *Economic Review*, October 1891.

THE RIGHTS OF THE INDIVIDUAL

principle of Equality of Consideration, and therefore
I will not dwell upon the subject further now. I will
confine myself to simply pointing out its bearing upon
our present question of the rights of the individual as
against society. If our principle be sound, the State
has no right to sacrifice the individual to the public
interest, if by that is meant that it may act in the way
that would be best for the public were that individual
out of the way. In a desert island, for instance, with
provisions running short, it might be highly convenient
for ten persons to distribute the provisions as though
there were only nine and to ignore the tenth, especially
if he were incapable of working and adding anything
to the common stock. That would violate the principle
of Equality of Consideration. On the other hand,
there may be occasions—in war, for instance—where
the public interest absolutely requires the sacrifice of
one life. To spare that one life and let all the people
perish would be no less a violation of Equality of
Consideration. The individual gets his rights, even
when he is shot, provided that, before it was decided to
send him on the forlorn hope or whatever it was, his interests were considered as much as those of anyone else.
Applying our principle, therefore, to the distribution
of wealth and the economic structure upon which that
distribution is dependent, we must hold that there is
no kind or amount of concrete inequality which may
not be justified if, under the circumstances, the system
is the one which is calculated to bring about the
greatest amount of good to distribute and the most
equal practicable distribution of that good. To secure
equality of actual possession, or of enjoyment, or of
social or political status at the cost of there being very
little to distribute for anyone would be the most
extreme of all possible violations of the principle of
Equality of Consideration. To introduce some social
or economic change which would have the ultimate
effect of bringing everyone down to the economic level
of the submerged tenth would be, in the abstract,

63

treating that tenth as if it were of as much importance as the whole, and, in the concrete, doing even that tenth no ultimate good at all.

Of the many difficulties which suggest themselves in connection with this doctrine, there is just one upon which I should like briefly to dwell. So long as all men are equally capable of well-being, and of the same sort of well-being, the principle of equality strikes us, I think, as self-evidently just and reasonable. But how if some men are not capable of the highest well-being, and if the higher well-being of the few costs the community much more than the lower well-being of the many? Which is to be preferred—the production of a little of the highest kind of life or of a great deal of an inferior kind of life? Ought, for instance, art and literature and learning to be sacrificed to a wider distribution of commonplace comfort and a low general intelligence? I must content myself with giving you, baldly and dogmatically, my own answer to the question. I should certainly say that the quality of well-being is to be given its proper weight as well as quantity, and I should not limit the notion of superior quality to strictly moral superiority. Equality of Consideration means simply that the same kind of life is of equal intrinsic value whether it be mine or yours. In regard to the mutual relation of various classes in the same race or community, I do not think that this qualification is of much practical importance; for the maintenance of culture and learning will be generally admitted to be for the real higher and ultimate good even of classes which do not directly or immediately participate in such higher goods of life. Of course, there may be much culture of a certain kind that really does not do anything for society. For the maintenance of such a culture I should certainly decline to make sacrifices of lower general welfare; a selfish or anti-social culture is no part of the true good even of the individuals that possess it. When, however, we turn from the relation between class and class in a homogeneous nation to the relation between race and race, then I should be quite prepared to contend that legislation which favoured the substitution of one European or American citizen with a European standard of life for two negroes or two Chinamen was amply justified. I do not contemplate, of course, legislation which would actually ill-treat or starve existing negroes or Chinamen. I am merely thinking of such restrictions on immigration as will have the effect of preventing competition between a higher and a lower race of a kind which would ultimately, if unrestricted, have the effect of reducing the general standard of life for the higher race and of favouring the multiplication of the lower. It must be remembered, however, that ultimately even the lower races of mankind may derive some benefit from such unequal fostering of the higher kind of life. For if the lower or backward races of mankind are ever to be participators in the civilisation and culture of the higher it can only be by the maintenance in unimpaired vigour of the higher type.

Our general conclusion then is that the rights of the individual are such rights as it can be shown to be desirable that he should possess in the interest of general well-being, general well-being to be interpreted according to the principle of Equality of Consideration. There is no concrete, specific liberty of action or of acquisition which may not under some circumstances be inconsistent with the general well-being. We cannot say that a man has an absolute right to work or to the necessaries of life, or to marry and have children, or anything of the kind, because under certain circumstances the benefit which such a general concession would secure to the few would be purchased by the wrong of a vastly greater number. This seems to be the consideration that is ignored by the attempts of many writers on political philosophy or natural law to draw up a list in detail of the various rights of action and acquisition which the State should under all circumstances secure to its subjects. The most that such efforts can really succeed in doing is to formulate some of the principal liberties of action and acquisition which experience has shown to be most generally and unmistakably conducive to general well-being at the stage of moral and material development hitherto reached by the more forward Western nations. But in strictness there is no right that may not, under some circumstances, have to give way to the general interest; while the most artificial and detailed clause in a Factory Act which can be shown to involve a practicable addition to the sum of human well-being may be quite as much claimed as an indefeasible part of the rights of man as all vague and high-sounding liberties which form the substance of philosophic systems of natural right. In exact strictness of speech, there is but one indefeasible right of man—the right to consideration.

And here, perhaps, it may be well to say a word as to a version of the rights of man which has of late acquired great popularity—that known as equality of opportunity. Equality of opportunity is, no doubt, a very attractive catch-word. It commends itself to Socialists by its democratic and levelling sound. It takes the ear of the Individualist by the alluring prospect which holds out to him that, even in Utopia, it will still be open to him to win great prizes by his superior agility in climbing upon his brother's shoulders; while even the suggestion that the allotment of wealth will still be partly governed by the caprices of fortune has its attractions for the many minds which feel quite a disinterested aversion to a world in which nobody will be very rich and have a really good time. Nor will I deny that, as a practical maxim, the formula has its merits. Undoubtedly we do want, at least in certain directions, much more equality of opportunity than we have got at present. Undoubtedly it would be a real benefit to society if the more capable members of the poorer classes were given increased facilities for rising to the higher social functions, while the less

capable members of the privileged classes were given
increased facilities for descending, say, to the game-
keeping and horse-grooming functions for which alone
they possess any moral or intellectual qualifications.
But taken as an exact and philosophic statement of an
indefeasible right of humanity, I must maintain that
equality of opportunity is as big an impostor as any
of the rights of man contained in the code of the late
" Mr. Midshipman Easy."

Equality of opportunity, on our principles, can only
be accepted as a right of man in proportion as it can
be shown to be really conducive to the general good.
And it is a mere assumption to suppose that equality
of opportunity is always and everywhere for the
general good. I doubt, indeed, whether unlimited
equality of opportunity will ever be practicable, or
whether even so far as it is practicable, it will ever be
really for the general good. But we will leave Utopias
for the present, and confine ourselves to the society of
the nineteenth and twentieth centuries. In any state
of society to which we can at present even aspire, I
believe that a certain considerable inequality of opportunity will continue to be for the general good As a
rule, speaking very broadly and roughly, and allowing
for large exceptions, men are best fitted—not always,
of course, for the exact trade—but for the same sort
of employment as their fathers. Such a doctrine does
not necessarily imply a marked inequality in average
capacity of a strictly intellectual type between different
classes in society. It is not necessarily a question of
superior intellectual power, but of superior adaptability
and capacity for particular kinds of work. As a rule,
the son of a doctor will make a better doctor, clergyman, or higher-grade teacher than the son of an
artisan. He will do better in the profession—not
merely get on better, but do its work better—than a
man of somewhat superior brain power who has been
born and educated among manual workers. And at
manual work the artisan's son will beat the professional

man's. Or again, little as I am given to ecstatic admiration of our hereditary aristocracy, I would even admit that *ceteris paribus* the man of blue blood will make a better diplomat than the son of an ordinary professional man; though here I must add that the advantage is one which is very soon neutralised by real intellectual and educational superiority. It is at second-rate statesmanship or second-rate diplomacy that the aristocrat excels. Superior capacity or adaptability of this kind is, no doubt, very largely and mainly a matter of early training and social environment. But it is just possible—Weismannism notwithstanding—that it is to some small extent a matter of direct inheritance. There is, I believe, a saying in Lancashire that it takes three generations to make a cotton-spinner; and it is alleged that the superior manners and address of sons of so-called gentlemen assert themselves very decidedly in orphanages where they are brought up in exactly the same way and amid exactly the same surroundings as the children of the poorest. On the whole, then, it seems best that, as in the Platonic Commonwealth, the sons should, as a rule, follow the same kind or sort of occupation as the father, while we undoubtedly want to provide increased means of promotion for really superior capacity, and facilities for kicking downstairs the unfit—the unfit specimens, chiefly of the wealthiest classes, which certain public schools seem specially constructed to manufacture. Undoubtedly we should gain by having more doctors and clergymen and lawyers taken from the more promising members of the working-class, provided, of course, they received an equally good education, than from the less promising members—I will not say of the upper classes (that monopoly having been more or less broken down), but I will say of the collar-wearing classes. Still it is very doubtful whether the community would benefit by having *all* its doctors selected by competitive examination from a community enjoying complete equality of educational opportunity.

Up to a certain point the tact, the manners, the knowledge of the world, the superficial culture that is an
affair of breeding rather than of books or of morals in
any higher sense—up to a certain point superiority in
these things will often make the average man of the
higher class a more useful doctor or teacher or clergyman than his moral and intellectual superior from a
lower class. So long as this is so, inequality of opportunity is demanded by social well-being, and
equality of opportunity is no right of man.

It will be said, of course, that these things may be
true while the present inequalities continue, but that
all this will be altered when the highest education and
the best manners have ceased to be the monopolies of a
class. To this I answer:

i. It can never, even in Utopia, be desirable to give
the highest intellectual education to every capable
member of the manual-labouring class. A good share
of the highest intellectual capacity is wanted in the
general interest for many of what are now considered
lower occupations, but not the highest intellectual culti-
vation. The exceptionally skilful artisan would
probably make a good artist or engineer, but it would
not be at all desirable to give every child capable of
becoming a good artisan the opportunity of becoming
an artist or an engineer; for society wants good
artisans quite as much—and wants more of them—
than good artists or engineers. A good police super-
intendent may bring to bear upon his work the qualities
which, with education, would have made a good cabinet
minister; but, if we give every child with such potentia-
lities the opportunity of becoming an educated politician and competing for a seat in the Cabinet, we shall
have none but inferior police superintendents; and yet
it is quite as important to society to have good police
superintendents as to have good cabinet ministers. I
believe there is a general tendency greatly to exaggerate the rareness of the ability that is wanted for high
professional or administrative or political work. Every

college tutor knows of ten men fit to be cabinet ministers for every one who will ever have the chance of becoming a cabinet minister. Genius, of course, is rare, but then we cannot always expect genius even in our Prime Ministers. Only three or four statesmen, I suppose, in the whole course of English history have been men of genius.

ii. Some will be found to reply that the superior attractiveness of the intellectual professions depends largely upon a conventional estimate of their superior respectability, and upon the superior remuneration actually attaching to them. With the disappearance of class prejudice, it will be said, the exceptionally skilled artisan will consider himself on a level with the successful doctor or politician, and there will be no undue competition for the latter occupations. I reply:

a. I do not in the least believe this to be the case. That a man endowed with conspicuous mental power and corresponding moral capacities will not think it a nobler thing—a more attractive sphere for his energies —to rule his fellow-men, to manage a government department or a great industrial concern, to conduct scientific investigations, or to write books, than to cut glasses, to make a particular corner of a particular machine, or to carry out the detailed drudgery of subordinate administration—that is to me, I must confess, utterly incredible. And yet gifts may be required to cut glasses and make machines—to say nothing of suggesting detailed mechanical improvements which nobody will think of but the actual workman, or, again, to regulate labour movements—which, with a more elaborate intellectual education, would make a leading doctor or a learned historian. The feeling will be just as strong if cabinet ministers should hereafter live in model buildings and wear corduroy. There will always, as it seems to me, be vastly more people capable of performing the highest social functions than there are highest social functions for them to perform.

Within certain limits it is, no doubt, socially healthy that there should be a competition for such places. But to give large masses of persons an education which necessarily and inevitably awaken's ambitions which cannot be satisfied, and tastes which cannot be gratified, and so to increase their discontent with that drudgery which must inevitably form a large portion of the lives of the majority, though, of course, it never ought to form the whole—such a policy does seem to me, I confess, to involve a most gratuitous increase in the sum of human misery. And yet that would be the inevitable result of a logical application of the principle of equality of opportunity.

b. So much seems to me clear, even apart from the differences of remuneration in different classes and the consequent differences in the standard of comfort. Personally, I am disposed to believe that there must always be in a healthy society differences in the remuneration of different kinds of work—vastly smaller differences than at present; yet differences in the remuneration of *work,* for of course I am not defending the present preponderant remuneration of idleness. But, however that may be, these differences exist. And, as long as they exist, they must necessarily be shared by the families of the various classes. If your superior individual or your superior trade is to receive differential renumeration, the sons of such privileged persons, however inferior in character or capacity, must necessarily share the superior comfort and culture of the father's home, unless you are prepared for a Socialism which will practically involve the abolition of the family. If so, it needs little argument to show that it would not conduce to the general well-being that the son of a doctor should have no better opportunity of becoming a doctor himself than the son of an artisan. If his intellectual capacity falls below a certain level, he should (ideally) descend in the social scale: it does not follow that he should descend in actual proportion to his intellectual capacity; the very fact of his having

71

been brought up as a doctor's son will, except in the extremest cases, have fitted him for some things which the average son of the average labourer would do less well.

I do not think it necessary to draw out in any detail either the impossibility or the inconveniences of such an ideal—the ideal of absolutely equal opportunity—understood in its literal fullness. It may be replied that at all events this is the direction in which we ought to move; that the ideal is unattainable, but that we can approximate to it, while there is not the least danger of our approximating to it too closely under existing conditions. I am quite ready to accept the motto "*Towards* equality of opportunity" as a convenient formulation of quite reasonable social aspirations. Still, I think it is worth while to point out that there is a very appreciable danger that we may be misled by this ideal of equality of opportunity in certain particular directions. If we could really, under existing economic conditions, give the poor man's promising son as good a chance of successfully embracing a profession as the average son of the upper- or upper-middle-class family, there might be much to be said in favour of such a scheme. But the danger is that we may equalise one set of conditions without equalising the rest. It is very easy by means of an extensive system of scholarships to give a large number of promising pupils from elementary schools the chance of continuing their education up to seventeen. Even these will not, probably, be the absolutely ablest; it will be only a minority who can afford, even with a scholarship, to stay at school up to seventeen. But the difficulty is to provide them with any career which will give them half as good a chance of using their abilities to their own advantage and that of the community as they would have had if apprenticed to a good trade at fourteen. When the ladder is extended to the universities, the difficulty becomes even greater. A few scholarships of that kind, sufficiently few to limit them to boys of really remarkable ability, are a good thing. For the very exceptional boy there are openings, but not for large numbers who might be quite capable of winning scholarships. We may easily have too many of such scholarships—too many, in the interest both of the boys themselves and of society. I should not object to a further extension of such schemes, though I think there are more certainly remunerative openings for social enterprise, if only the private benefactors or public authorities would make provision for the employment as well as for the education of such scholarship-holding boys from elementary schools. But, so long as that is not done, there is a real danger of the system being carried too far. It is forgotten that the English universities are not, to any large extent, places of professional education. A man who has taken a degree in Arts at Oxford or Cambridge can earn his living immediately in only three ways—as a schoolmaster or as a clergyman, or now, happily (with fairly good ability), as an Indian Civilian. It is very undesirable to increase the number of persons who are thrown upon the world at twenty-three with only these alternatives before them—for all of which, in many cases, there may be some fatal disqualification.

Of course I know that these remarks will raise all sorts of indignant protests from persons whom one may perhaps without offence describe as Idealists in education. I confess that I do hold to the old-fashioned opinion of Plato, that everyone should be educated with some view to the kind of work in life which he will have to do. At the same time, I hasten to add that I have every sympathy with the effort to provide the best possible elementary education for all, to extend its age as much as shall be found practicable, and to give to all after the school age is over the opportunity in their leisure hours of acquiring knowledge for its own sake to the fullest extent to which they have any appetite for it. But, for all that, I do hold that it is not socially desirable to extend the principle of equality of opportunity in its fullest extent to the distribution of work among those who have to do it and that the extension of educational opportunities should to some extent keep pace with the extension of the professional opportunities which lie beyond them.

I come back to the main doctrine which it is the object of this paper to enforce. Except the right to equality of consideration there is no right in the individual which does not spring from the demands of social well-being. So long as this principle of equality of consideration is respected, there is no possible extension of State interference which can be reasonably resisted in the name of the individual's rights. Such an admission may seem to some to lead us very far indeed in the direction of Socialism. Perhaps in some ways it does. How far State interference should be carried, how far such interference really is conducive to that general well-being which is the source and criterion of all rights, I do not know. That is a matter which growing experience alone can determine. I should attach little importance to any surmises of mine as to the extent to which such intervention is likely to prove successful, and I should attach scarcely more importance on that subject to the guesses of any other man. But one thing must be said on behalf of the claims of the individual who is threatened on all sides by the advances of Socialism in theory and in practice. It must not be forgotten that this State, whose abstract right to interfere with any and every department of social life is so undeniable, after all consists of individuals. The success or failure of every kind of State action must ultimately depend upon the moral and intellectual qualities of the individuals who direct it. Any system, therefore, which is unfavourable to the growth of the best possible individuals can never be socially beneficial. The degeneration of the individual must inevitably lead to the degeneration of the society which is composed of individuals, and whose moral and intellectual level cannot possibly rise higher than that of

74

the best-developed individuals within it. Now, there is a real danger that the increase of State interference may actually lead to the extinction of character. Faculties that cannot be used become atrophied. If society is to be composed of persons accustomed to feel that their work in life, the time that they are to work, the food that they are to eat, the houses that they are to live in, the amusements that they have to look forward to, their comfort in old age, the future of their children will all be provided for them entirely irrespective of any effort or exertion of theirs, beyond what is implied in obeying the law and coming up to the average standard of industrial efficiency—how in such persons is character to be developed? Character depends upon responsibility. It is no use to say that the citizen will find employment for his energies in the service of society and for his affections in the love of it. Character is developed by acts of choice; a state of things where hardly anything depends upon the choice of the individual cannot be favourable either to the intellectual or the moral development of human nature. Thus persons not educated by responsibility for the lives of themselves and their families will never be fit to direct the energies of a community. There must, therefore, be a limit to State interference in the interest of human character, no matter what success there may be in overcoming the material difficulties of the Collectivist programme. Exactly where that limit must be placed I do not, of course, attempt to decide. But meanwhile it will be enough for the guidance of our present social policy that we should observe exactly where the danger of injury to character by State intervention really begins. For the State to do for people things that they cannot possibly do for themselves has no demoralising tendency whatever. Now, with regard to most of the recently accomplished or proposed pieces of legislation which move the wrath of Individualist critics, it is admitted that this is the case. The very gravamen against such interferences is that they are artificially securing to the poor decencies, comforts, luxuries, culture, amusements, sanitation of a kind which poor men could not possibly provide for themselves—artificially putting the poor man in certain respects on a level with the rich man. The danger begins just when we begin to do for the poor man the things which the industrious, capable, reasonably self-controlled poor man can and does now do for himself, —when we teach him to think that, no matter how little trouble he may take to get work and keep work when he has got it, to earn money and not to spend it too soon, he and those dependent on him are pretty sure to be able to fall back upon a minimum subsistence, earned without labour or by casual and irregular labour subject to no really onerous or irksome conditions. I will leave it to your experience to apply what I have said to concrete cases. I will only remind you in a general way that the kind of demoralisation which might be apprehended from certain kinds of Collectivism is quite equally within the reach of private philanthropy. The only direct application of what I have said upon which I will venture will be to say, that in the immediate future there is far more danger of demoralising Collectivism in attempts to provide food and work for the residuum, whether by State action or by wholesale charity, than there is in attempts to improve the wages, conditions of labour, and conditions of existence for those who are really entitled to be called the working classes.

I do not intend, however, to be led astray into any general discussion of the question of Socialism. If there were any practical lesson which I would wish to extract from the purely theoretical inquiry on which we have been engaged, it would be the inadvisability of busying ourselves overmuch at present with the question of ultimate schemes of social reorganisation. I have tried simply to lay down three principles:

1. That the individual's only absolute right is Equality of Consideration.

2. That the State has an absolute right to interfere with the individual to any extent conducive to the general good, interpreted in accordance with the principle of Equality of Consideration.

3. That the development of individual character is in itself of primary importance, in enabling the State to do whatever it undertakes to do—whether little or much—for the promotion of that highest well-being, or good life, for which it exists.

V

THE IDEA OF PROGRESS [1]

I NEED not begin this paper by paying compliments to the brilliancy of the lecture which supplies the starting-point of our discussion. Indeed, my chief complaint against the lecture as a serious contribution to thought is that it is too brilliant. " Dark with excess of light " is the phrase which is constantly recalled to me by this and other writings of the same author. It is a little difficult to make out exactly what is the thesis which the Dean of St. Paul's aims at establishing. There is no doubt, indeed, about the nature of the idols which he is smashing; and there is no doubt that, so long as he confines himself to the congenial task of iconoclasm, Dr. Inge's contentions are in the main sound. I have no inclination to defend the doctrine that there is a " law of progress " in human affairs whether in its Spencerian or its Hegelian form or in the form of that popular Optimism which the Dean associates with a certain portion of the Nineteenth Century, and which is no doubt not altogether dead yet. I do not know of any *a priori* ground for saying that the world must necessarily be progressing on the whole—still less that each age must necessarily be in any sense better than the last, least of all that the progress must be of indefinite duration or that it must culminate in some terrestrial millennium.

But on the positive side I find it a little difficult to find the exact thesis which Dr. Inge aims at establishing. I hope I shall not be misinterpreting him in taking him to maintain these two propositions:

(1) That there has been no progress in the past; and (2) that it is unreasonable to expect any progress in the future, though we are not positively forbidden to hope for it.

At all events, whether maintained by the Dean or not, these are propositions which I am prepared to meet

[1] A paper in criticism of the Dean of St. Paul's Romanes Lecture (reprinted in *Outspoken Essays,* Second Series).

78

with a direct negative. But let me explain the limitations with which I take the two propositions. I confine myself for the present to the history of this planet. I have nothing to do with any speculations as to the progress of the Universe as a whole—whether a self-improvement of " the Absolute " or an improvement of all finite spirits in the Universe; and, on the other hand, I do not maintain that even on this planet progress may be expected to go on indefinitely. I shall not busy myself with any speculations as to the ultimate future whether of the cosmic process or even of this earth; I will merely remark that I believe Physicists are not absolutely unanimous as to the dismal future which Dr. Inge assumes to be in store for the human race; and I suppose that it is always possible that, even if that prediction is on physical grounds well established, a gradual extinction of life through excessive cold may be averted by some cosmic catastrophe. I shall simply try to offer some grounds for these two modest propositions: (1) On the whole there has been progress on this planet—no doubt with many lapses, periods of stagnation, and periods of retrogression. (2) There is a reasonable expectation of such progress being continued for a considerable period in the future.

It would no doubt be well to start with some definition of progress. Such a definition Dr. Inge has steadily refused to give. But I do not know that we should differ very seriously as to our general conception of what progress would be if there were any such thing. By progress I mean an increase of all that is valuable—an increase in quality and quantity taken together. As to what things are valuable there would probably not be much difference of opinion between us so long as we confine ourselves to generalities; though in detail I should be disposed to find a value in many things which appear to fill my friend Dr. Inge with mere horror and disgust. " Our ultimate aim," he says, " is in the knowledge and enjoyment of the absolute values, Truth, Goodness, and Beauty." I can cordially accept that statement, though I would add two—I will not say qualifications of it—but interpretations of it, or, if it be so, additions to it. (1) I cannot conceive of an ideal life from which pleasure is absent. Dr. Inge appears to suggest it under cover of the word "enjoyment": I should be a little more candid. I recognise that the highest and most valuable kind of pleasure is that which springs from the knowledge and enjoyment of Truth, Goodness, and Beauty. But I am not prepared to deny all value to lower kinds of human pleasure; nor can I regard as wholly valueless, however low we place them, the lives of creatures whose joys cannot well be supposed to have much to do with Truth, Goodness, or Beauty. And (2) I should emphasise a little more the fact that Goodness is not a mere passive enjoyment of anything, but an activity of the will.

Now, as to the first of these propositions—that there has been progress—Dr. Inge introduces an important qualification to his otherwise sweeping negative. He declares that we are

"driven to the conclusion that neither science nor history gives us any warrant for believing that humanity has advanced, except by accumulating knowledge and experience and the instruments of living";[1]

and he attaches great value to this advance. This is so vast an admission that it reduces the limits of his original thesis to rather small proportions. The life of the modern man taken altogether apart from his increased knowledge and experience and his greater command of "the instruments of living" is surely a mere abstraction. We cannot abstract the conscious life, which increase of knowledge and experience and better instruments of living make possible, from the *conditions* which make it possible. Knowledge of the art of writing made possible literature of a higher

[1] *Outspoken Essays* (Second Series), p. 175.

80

and certainly more varied kind than that which consisted in extemporised or remembered ballad; the invention of printing enriches the life of millions who but for it would have had no books. That Dr. Inge believes in the value of literature for the few I do not doubt; personally I think that the life of the modern working man who can read is intrinsically more valuable than it was before that invention, even though the literature that he reads may be confined to *Lloyd's Newspaper* or the *Daily Herald*: here I am not so sure that Dr. Inge would follow me.

So again on the moral side, the man who believes that men—that is to say, the members of certain societies—are on the average better than their remote ancestors, does not necessarily imply that each individual would be better if you isolated him as an infant from all the influences of his society; that if you took an English infant and brought him up among savages, either his ideals or his practice would be conspicuously higher than that of the savages about him. " Knowledge and experience " will cover most of the influences by which men are made better or worse—example, precept, personal influence, law, tradition, social environment—the ideals of the past, the ideals of the present—the influence of school and home, of political and ecclesiastical institutions, of literature and oratory and education and all the manifold forms in which human beings communicate their ideas to one another. Language itself is a form of accumulated knowledge and experience, though it implies a certain physical development. The isolated man, it is a philosophical commonplace to deny, is an unreal abstraction. When the consequences of Dr. Inge's enormous admission are thought out, his denial of progress seems to be reduced to the modest assertion that the modern man, as he comes naked from his mother's womb, is not intrinsically cleverer or better than his remote ancestor of the Palaeolithic Age. This is an assertion to deal satisfactorily with which much

F

biological and other knowledge would be required. But I think that there is a way of attacking the subject which need not raise disputed questions about the inheritance of acquired characteristics and the like.

If we go back far enough, we must needs come to a period up to which the fact of progress can hardly be disputed—even of progress in the actual nature and capacities of the human animal when isolated from the whole of his social inheritance. Even Dr. Inge will hardly be disposed to deny that the intelligence of what are commonly called the higher animals is higher than that of the lower; and I at least do not feel disposed to doubt that the pleasure accompanying this more intelligent consciousness is of some value. The lives of dogs and cats and elephants seem to me of more value than the kind of consciousness which we may suppose to exist in worms and amoebae or whatever you may suppose to be the first animals endowed with consciousness. And the most evanescent sensation of a butterfly has a worth which there is no convincing reason to attribute to anything in the life even of the cedar or the rose. And the life of the highest sub-human creatures must surely have been more intelligent and more valuable than that of dogs and cats. I cannot suppose that the value of all these myriads of conscious beings was wholly that of means to the evolution of man. And I see no reason to believe that this increase of value stops just where you choose to fix the limit between the sub-human and the human. Dr. Inge tells us that men of the old Stone Age, ugly as most of them must have been (here, by the way, there seems an admission of *some* progress), " had as large brains as ours "; but I have always understood that the size of the brain was, by itself, a very insufficient test of intellectual capacity. Does Dr. Inge seriously suppose that palaeolithic man was in intellectual capacity the equal of Plato and his circle—even apart from their small inheritance of acquired knowledge, experience, and instruments of living? Certainly all analogy is

82

against that view. Does he suppose that among the lowest of existing races—the natives of Central Australia, for instance—there are many or even any individuals capable of being educated up to the level of an Oxford or Cambridge First-classman or the morally first-class modern man? If not, there must have been progress, at least between the time of the monkey and that of Plato. All the evidence that Dr. Inge produces in support of his no-progress theory comes to this—that the intellectual capacity of the classical Greek period was as high as that of ourselves. The 2,300 years between Socrates and ourselves is a small period in the development of the human species. Before this, at least, there must have been a real advance in the actual intellectual and moral capacity of the human race; and in the vast majority of the human race that progress must have been continued since then, since it was only a tiny fraction of the race who can be supposed to have reached the level of the Greeks. And then, after all, the question of the actual native capacity of different races or ages is, as I have suggested, really quite irrelevant to this question of progress. Whatever the native capacity of the big-brained old Stone-age man may have been, it can hardly be denied that the life of man at that period was, in Hobbes's language, " solitary, poor, nasty, brutish, and short ": the " solitary " is the only element in this estimate which need be put down mainly to the requirements of Hobbes's *a priori* theories. The higher life of man would be more valuable none the less than the lower because (even if it were true) most of the differences may be traceable to the larger inheritance of knowledge, experience, and instruments of living.

When we return to a more natural mode of estimating progress, the question becomes less capable of anything like scientific proof. It is difficult here to avoid the influence of subjective prejudices. Dr. Inge's estimates of value seem to be distorted by his extreme dislike of democracy and his terror of the assaults made or contemplated by the British working man (upon the dividends of the class which Dr. Inge always regards as possessing a monopoly of high culture, the owners of capital. I perhaps, though by no means an unqualified enthusiast for democracy, may be equally biased by a certain dislike of the Absolutisms and Aristocracies which seem to be nearing their fall, and a certain sympathy with the masses of people who, after centuries of oppression and under-payment, are now beginning to be better off. None of us can wholly escape the influence of the personal equation. We can only do our best.

Upon Dr. Inge's treatment of the question of progress within the historical period I would make the following remarks:

(1) It is characteristic of his mode of thought that Dr. Inge looks at the whole human panorama from the aristocratic point of view. He estimates the level of the land entirely by measuring the highest peaks. Because Plato's genius in Philosophy has not been equalled, therefore the accumulated labours of the mere Leibnizes and Kants, the mere Berkeleys and Bradleys, do not constitute an advance in Philosophy. Still less does it matter to him what sort of life was lived by Plato's slaves or by the millions who lay outside the extremely limited circle who were capable of reading and appreciating Plato. What most of us would account great steps of human progress—the decay of cruel and cramping superstitions, with the misery of which Sir James Frazer has familiarised us, the abolition of slavery over the greater part of the earth's surface, the vast increase in the number of persons who can read and write and enjoy the elementary culture which these instruments of living secure, the enormous increase in human happiness and (I think one may add) self-respect which have followed the French Revolution and the Factory Acts—such things

84

as these do not seem to him worthy of mention. This aristocratic attitude comes out conspicuously in the following sentence:

"If it is progress to turn the fields and woods of Essex into East and West Ham, we may be thankful that progress is a sporadic and transient phenomenon in history." [1]

Surely the vanished fields and woods of Essex were not an end-in-themselves: it is only so far as they were contemplated and enjoyed by someone that they had any value at all. Because the fields and woods of Essex were a more beautiful spectacle to the aesthetic contemplator of them than monotonous rows of red-brick houses, therefore no progress can be traced in the change which has replaced them by the million or so of people, very few of whom, it is probable, ever read Plato or Plotinus. Yes! I do not regard it as a *reductio ad absurdum* to contend that there is value even in the life of East and West Ham. I should gather from the Dean's more edifying works that, though he is inclined to accuse of an ethical obsession those who place the value of Culture below that of Morality, he does attach a high value to the effort after righteousness, to religious faith, to love. There is reason to believe that much honest work is done in East and West Ham. There is family life and family affection. There is courting and there is marrying; and sometimes these marriages are happy. There are schools and schoolmasters, and they have pupils. There are, I doubt not, books, and men who read them, and even young men's mutual improvement societies, and W.E.A. classes, and perhaps a philosophical society, though it is possible that its gods are Mr. Spencer and Mr. H. G. Wells rather than Plato and Plotinus. I for one am not prepared to deny to these things a value greatly exceeding that of the vanished fields and woods or even of the occasional moments of aesthetic

[1] *Outspoken Essays* (Second Series), p. 167.

elation and philosophic reflection with which they may have inspired an occasional wanderer from the great city—a Dr. Donne or an Izaak Walton—in that idyllic period when trades-unions were not and working men were kept in their proper place. Coarse and prosaic as the notion may appear to Dr. Inge, I submit that quantity as well as quality must be taken into account in estimating the value of the world's conscious life at any period.

(2) I should like to comment on Dr. Inge's curious attitude towards the Middle Ages. He is far above the Eighteenth Century philistinism or ignorance which dismissed all the great historians of the Middle Ages as monkish scribblers and the Scholastic period as one in which the human mind simply marked time but made no advance. He recognises the distinction between the Dark Ages and the Middle Ages. And yet he can only see in the whole period up to the Renaissance "the longest and dreariest set-back that humanity has ever experienced within the historical period." (How, by the way, can there be "set-backs" if there has not been progress on the whole?) And he estimates that seven centuries might be cut out of history without any great loss to posterity. (Here again he yields to his habit of treating whole generations as if their value consisted solely in the amount of satisfaction which can be got out of them in the backward glance of some philosophic contemplator of all time and all existence.) I don't gather exactly when Dr. Inge makes his seven dark centuries begin; but if we take as the earliest possible date 500 and make them last to 1200, he will have cut out nearly all the books of Roman Law which are still studied by lawyers and which govern the life of half the civilised world, many of the great works of the Romanesque and Norman Architecture, all the brilliant Mohammedan-Greek culture which spread from the School of Bagdad, and the beginnings of the Scholastic Philosophy and Theology—to say nothing of the vernacular

86

literature, which makes such a man as Professor Ker say that there were no Dark Ages. If we make the set-back last to the very earliest possible date for the beginning of the Renaissance, Dante and the greatest Gothic churches and the earlier Italian and Flemish painters will have to go by the board. But, whatever we may think of the permanent value to humanity of the products of this period, it was assuredly not all a period of stagnation or retrogression. The four hundred years to Charles the Great with somewhat of a set-back again for a generation or two after him is the longest period which can possibly be thus dismissed. From 1000 at the very latest progress began again; and, though much of the progress doubtless went to merely recovering the ground that had been lost, I cannot believe that any serious student of the Middle Ages, unless his anti-ecclesiastical prejudices are very strong, will deny that—whether we think of their intrinsic value or of their contribution to the world's future—there was in Medieval Civilisation much which was as valuable as (or in advance of) anything produced by those "notable flowering-times of the Spirit of Man," those short periods of very brilliant but highly exclusive and aristocratic culture upon which Dr. Inge's eyes are so almost exclusively fixed. Indeed, I am not sure that I should not be disposed to regard the Thirteenth Century as one such flowering-time. It is strange, too, that Dr. Inge of all people should dismiss so cavalierly centuries which produced so many of those Mystics who rouse him to an enthusiasm which I cannot pretend to share.

Not, indeed, that I am at all inclined to idealise the Middle Ages. Intellectually I believe they are far greater than is popularly supposed; to say nothing of their Art and their Philosophy and their Poetry, the Middle Ages created all the greatest institutions of the modern world—Representative government, Parliaments, Universities, Juries. But morally they have been overpraised. The saints were few—at least the

saints of orthodoxy; the highest moral and religious
life of the Middle Ages was probably on the whole
that of the heretics. It is scarcely possible to exaggerate the lowness of the average moral standard. Indeed, the best cure that I can recommend for pessi-
mism of Dr. Inge's type would be a course of really
first-hand study of medieval documents. The horrors
perpetrated by the Germans at Louvain or by the
agents of the present government in Ireland—the
outbreaks of modern " frightfulness " which no doubt
offer the biggest difficulties to any complacent view
about the moral progress of the world—were simply
the every-day incidents of medieval history. Saints
and sinners alike took them as a matter of course, and
saints were directly responsible for some of the worst
of them. At the present day large numbers of people
are at least capable of being shocked by them. It is
not only on the defects of the medieval ideals or the
imperfections of its rare saints that I would insist:
I cannot doubt that the average modern man is in
matters of ordinary, every-day morality enormously
above the moral level of the average medieval. In the
medieval world grave adults in every rank of life quar-
relled and fought on the slightest provocation like
small boys at a private school or the roughest and
coarsest classes of the present day. There was an
astounding absence of the most ordinary self-control.
Anybody who had charge of money was usually suspected of peculation; and no doubt the suspicion was
often not groundless. Every reader of Chaucer
knows something of the lowness of the sexual level;
but there is much more behind. Murder was as common as petty theft is to-day. The Proctors at Oxford
were required to keep lists of homicides who had
been banished from the University, and were mostly
(it is probable) studying at Cambridge: for murder,
as a rule, involved only a change of residence. Doubtless the Cambridge Proctors kept a similar list. I
am not professing to speak with any statistical accur-

acy, but the general impression that one gets from medieval records is that there must have been as many murders in the scantily-populated medieval England in a week as there are now in a year, and the violent assaults must have been in proportion.

Looking at the whole course of human history, I cannot doubt (though I cannot really claim the knowledge to make so vast a generalisation) that, if you take a sufficiently wide sweep, there has been progress in the world from the first dawn of animal consciousness down to the present—a slow and gradual increase of values or valuable consciousness. This progress has not, indeed, been uniform, for there have been periods of great retrogression; there has been progress in one quarter while there has been retrogression in another: in the same country there has often been marked decline in one respect, great progress in another. The Fifteenth and Eighteenth Centuries will sufficiently illustrate what I mean. But on the whole the direction of evolution seems to be in the direction of greater value. And that fact is a sufficient basis for the belief that such progress will go on. It is surely not an unphilosophical procedure to estimate the general character of Reality from that part of it of which we have direct knowledge. I do not know any philosophy which does not at bottom do this, if we take into account the existence of ideals as well as of actualities. As to the inferences that may be drawn from the nature of our ideals, I will say a word in a minute; but, confining myself for the present to facts, I contend that it is reasonable to infer from the known facts that some of the characteristics of the Universe—or, if we prefer a more modest inference, of this planet—advance on the whole in the direction of a more valuable existence. That the progress will be of indefinite duration I do not assert; I merely contend that it is reasonable to expect a general improvement of human life upon this planet in the next few hundreds, probably thousands, of years.

So far, I have made no assumptions of a metaphysical character. But the argument is greatly strengthened for those who share the belief which Dr. Inge and I have in common as to the spiritual and moral character of the Ultimate Reality. On the assumption that our higher ideals reveal the character of the spiritual Being who is also in some sense revealed by the world-process, it is reasonable to infer that the world-process must be making for the realisation of those ideals. It may be asked, " Why should the end of the process reveal the character of that Being more than its earlier stages? " It might be sufficient to fall back once more upon experience, and say that according to our judgements of value the later stages of the process seem to contain more value than the earlier ones, and that therefore we must infer that the earlier are for the later rather than the later for the earlier. Moreover, in all processes which are due to rational activity means come first and the end last. The distinction between means and ends is not indeed a merely temporal distinction; it implies a distinction of values: the means are for the end as well as to the end. In processes which are due to rational volition, when the later stage of a process seems to have more value in it than the earlier, we infer that the earlier stages are willed as a necessary means to that higher value towards which the process is directed. Applying that inference to the world-process, we should infer that the big-brained Stone-age man, though he has some value in himself, is for the sake of Plato rather than Plato for the sake of the big-brained savage: and we may therefore infer not necessarily that a greater philosopher than Plato will one day appear, but that the later state of the planet will be on the whole better than the present. The conclusion is not absolutely necessary. There may be some reason in the nature of things why, at a certain stage in the life of this planet, life must deteriorate in value and ultimately disappear. If so, we should have to believe that increase of value which seems to contain the only rational explanation of the world-process may have to take place in some other planet than this, or in the continued life of individuals in some state for which the present is a necessary preparation. But the probabilities are enormously against the supposition that we have actually reached the limit of that increase of value upon this earth which can be traced up to this point.

To Dr. Inge this line of thought will not be convincing, for a very simple reason. He does not believe in time or in the validity of categories which imply time. You cannot believe in real progress if you do not believe in real time. But on his own supposition that final causes are the only real causes, I do not see why he should not recognise that an apparent progress is for minds which at least appear to be in time a more adequate representation of eternal Reality than apparent retrogression. From the temporal point of view the evils of an earlier stage in the time-process appear to be most rationally explained as a means to the good realised in the later; they would not be explained if they led up to a greater mass of evil than is involved in the earlier. A progressive world would therefore seem, even though only an appearance, a better revelation of the eternal nature of the Absolute than an unprogressive or retrogressive world; and we should therefore expect the Absolute to reveal Himself in an apparently progressive time-process. Why the Absolute should reveal Himself in so very misleading a way, why a timeless Absolute or God should disguise Himself in time, why there ever should be the appearance of a time-process, when in point of fact Reality is always static, changeless, and perfect, is a question which neither Dr. Inge, nor Plotinus, nor any other Philosophy which denies the reality of time has ever so much as attempted to explain. To that generalisation there is one possible exception: there is a well-known passage in Mr. Bradley in which it is suggested that human error is explained by the diversion which it affords to the Absolute. Perhaps the time-process is a huge joke. According to this view the time-process might be looked upon as a misleading appearance of Reality—an appearance whose value consists precisely in its misleading character. This would be an explanation as far as it goes; but it would imply of course an ascription to the Absolute of a character which a Christian Neo-platonist could not well adopt. It certainly would not be accepted by Dr. Inge, in spite of a passage or two in which minor eccentricities of the temporal world are accounted for as jokes expressive of an eternal and changeless sense of humour.

It is quite impossible at this point to enter upon any discussion of the time-problem. Forty years ago one could only venture to whisper the idea that time is real, and that God is in time in a very modest way if one wished to escape the consuming ridicule of one's philosophical friends. At the present moment it needs less apology. But I am far from thinking that to say " time is real " puts an end to all our difficulties. I am quite sure that it is nearer the truth to say that " time is real " than to say it is " unreal," or an appearance, or a delusion, or merely subjective. The first statement at least means something: the latter, to my mind, means nothing at all. The most that it can mean is the merely negative proposition that the temporal aspect of the Universe is not the only aspect— that to say that God is in time cannot be the whole truth about Him and His relation to the world. I do not deny that in some sense to a complete view of the world, time may be transcended; but I do not believe that the Kantian antinomy has been transcended by Hegel, by Mr. Bradley, or by anyone else. And therefore I do not think it is possible to solve those further problems as to the limits of progress or the end of the world-process to which the preceding discussion naturally leads on; the impossibility of answering them constitutes the chief strength of those who ridicule the idea of progress as in any way expressive of the true and ultimate nature of things. But of this I feel sure—that the world-process really means something, and that we get as near to the truth as our imperfect minds allow us to do when we think of the Universe as realising a good which once did not exist, and of the earlier and less valuable stages in the process as necessary to the later and more valuable. In that sense and to that extent the idea of progress seems to me not merely an empirically observed fact about a limited section of the time-process, but one which contains a clue to the nature of Reality.

VI

MODERNISM [1]

You have asked me to read a paper on " Modernism."
The term " Modernism " is used in its strict sense to
indicate a movement or a mode of thought which has
arisen within the last twenty or thirty years in the
bosom of the Roman Catholic Church, chiefly in Italy
and France. The term is also used in that wider and
more general sense which it has recently begun to
acquire among ourselves as meaning theological Liberalism in general. That being so, I think I had better
adopt a sort of middle course and try to put the
Modernist movement in its narrower sense into relation with that much wider Liberal Movement in the
Church, which is, to those who have eyes to see it, such
a vastly more important thing than the more purely
ecclesiastical controversies which seem, on a superficial view, to occupy a larger place in the theological
life of our time.

There has been in all ages a Liberal wing of the
Church. In all ages—except possibly the very darkest
in the Church's history—there have been Christian
teachers who have attempted to interpret Christian
doctrine in accordance with the best science of the
day, to welcome and adopt newly discovered truth, to
give up disproved errors, honestly to face intellectual
difficulties.

There were Liberals and anti-Liberals among the
Fathers, among the Schoolmen, among the Reformers,
among the theologians of all later periods. Very
notable since the days of that school of philosophical
theologians known as the Cambridge Platonists there
has always been a Liberal section in the Church of
England. And in a sense the tendency, though not
of course the positive doctrines, of Liberalism have
always been the same. But there is one feature which
somewhat sharply differentiates the Liberalism of

[1] A paper read to the Carlisle Clerical Society, May 27, 1918.

recent days from the older Liberalism. Modern Liberalism is essentially based upon the critical study of the Old and New Testaments. And of that critical study, in spite of the anticipations of modern results by the Seventeenth Century French Jesuit Simon and the French physician Astruc, in spite of the bold and original work of Bishop Colenso in England, Germany has been until quite recently the chief home. To appreciate the position of the Modernist School, it is above all necessary to understand its relation to German Liberal Protestantism.

Till towards the end of the Nineteenth Century the Roman Catholic clergy of France were hardly at all influenced by criticism or, indeed, by modern thought and learning of any kind. Till then the most learned Roman Catholic scholars were Germans, who could not altogether escape the intellectual influences of the Protestant world with which they were in such close contact, especially in the Universities where Professors of Catholic Theology lived and taught side by side with lay colleagues and Protestant theologians. It was the German Bishops and theologians who held out longest against Papal Infallibility. But in France the clergy were educated in seminaries—caught when quite young boys, given their secular education in the *Petit Séminaire,* taught their philosophy and theology in the *Grand Séminaire*; and the seminaries remained to a large extent hermetically sealed against the influences of their age. Yet, not altogether; for the intellectual tone (say) of the French Church was of course enlightened, liberal, modern when compared with the Church as it was in the Middle Ages or (still more) the Church as it is in Spain or Southern Italy or South America. But the influence of modern thought upon the minds of the clergy was apt to stop short at the point where something of modern philosophy, something of modern science, something of the modern attitude towards life in general, penetrated within the seminary walls. Yet their theology remained the

95

theology of the Seventeenth Century, and that theology differed only a little from the theology of the Thirteenth Century. The theology of the seminaries had learned nothing that was not known to Bossuet, except a very little tolerance and a great deal of Ultramontanism. The Scholastic Philosophy and the Scholastic Theology, it must be remembered, were the main studies of the future priest. To be a theologian meant to be learned in all those dogmatic and metaphysical controversies about which the typical English or German Protestant theologian knows next to nothing. Biblical studies held a very subordinate place, and were carried on in a completely traditional spirit.

Towards the end of the Nineteenth Century all this was rather suddenly altered. The best minds among the seminary professors seem almost simultaneously and independently to have turned aside from a Scholasticism which they felt to be obsolete, and to have become keenly interested in those critical and historical problems with which Protestant theologians were chiefly occupied. And of course this interest must have been more or less inspired by Protestant influence. It is true that the most distinguished of the French Modernists, M. Loisy, tells us that he was led to reject the traditional view of biblical inerrancy simply by his own independent study of the orthodox text-books with which he was supplied in the seminary. But when doubt was once aroused, the inquiring minds in France and Italy who wanted to carry their investigations further, had to avail themselves of the help afforded by previous inquirers, and for such help they naturally turned to the writings of German or French Protestants. The results at which they arrived were of course various. But one and all found it impossible to accept the traditional account of the date, authorship, origin, and historicity of the Old and New Testament Scriptures. The name " Modernist " came to be freely applied both to the more moderate and the more extreme of those who rejected the tradi-

96

tional views. And all alike found themselves more or
less in collision with the ecclesiastical authorities.
Under the relatively liberal and scholarly Leo XIII
the Modernists enjoyed a certain amount of toleration,
and the new opinions spread rapidly. There were
Bishops who favoured them. The Archbishop of Albi
made his seminary a nursery of Modernism, and there
were probably not many intelligent young priests in
France or North Italy who were not more or less
affected by them. But towards the end of the Pontificate of Leo XIII they received a great check by the
new definition of Inspiration. Hitherto the whole
question of what inspiration implied had been happily
left more or less vague by the ancient Councils, by the
Council of Trent, and even by Protestant Confessions
of Faith. Now a dogma was imposed upon the
Church of Rome compared with which to a modern
mind the acceptance of Papal Infallibility was mere
child's play. It was now, in 1893, declared that the
whole contents of Scripture—including of course what
we call the Apocrypha—were as much inspired as if
God were the author of the whole Scriptures, and that
they were free from all error. Anyone who denied
this was henceforth a Modernist and liable to condemnation as such. The Encyclical *Providentissimus
Deus,* which thus defied all modern learning, was
issued in the latter part of Leo's reign. Leo was succeeded by the pious but ignorant Venetian peasant,
Pius X, and under him a policy of downright persecution was inaugurated. An immense system of espi-
onage—worthy of Tiberius or Nero—was organised
for the detection of Modernist priests. No distinction was drawn between moderate Modernists and extreme ones. An oath disclaiming the Modernist
opinions could be imposed upon any priest. Those
who refused were liable to suspension and excommuni-
cation. A reign of terror set in. In spite of all these
efforts at repression, the Modernist leaders managed
to find ingenious ways of defending their position, and

G   97 carrying on their propaganda. In 1903 began a long series of condemnations. The Irish Jesuit Tyrrell was condemned in 1907; the French leader Loisy soon afterwards. I will not attempt to describe the measures taken against less eminent men. All Modernist priests had to choose between absolute silence and expulsion from the Roman fold. Modernist periodicals ceased to appear; Modernist books could no longer be published. Those who submitted, like the famous and eloquent Italian monk Semeria, were silenced—forbidden to preach or write or lecture, and compelled to occupy themselves with harmless functions such as the elementary education of children. The movement was crushed so far as any repression can crush a spiritual and intellectual revolution. Of course it is not to be supposed that the thousands of more or less Modernist priests had really changed their opinions. But they were rendered impotent. The propaganda could not be carried on—at least by the clergy. Seminarists could no longer be initiated into the mildest form of modern theological opinion. And the Modernists were likely to have few successors. Able and intelligent priests ceased to care to recruit for the priesthood. The suppression of Modernism and the disestablishment of the French Church (also the work of Pius X and the Curia) between them have gone nearly as far towards the suppression of the Catholic Church, and with it for the mass of Frenchmen of any organised expression of Religion, as it was well possible for the alliance between religious obscurantism and anti-Christian politics to go.

But it is time for me to turn now from the external history of the movement to its inner character. And particularly it is important to understand how far it differed from the Protestant Liberal theology, to which it owed more than it could well afford to acknowledge.

German theologians have not been, and are not, all Liberal, nor do all German Liberals agree among themselves. But the most powerful school of German theology—that which derives its inspiration and its name from the Göttingen Professor Ritschl—had certain tendencies which admit of being summarised in a fairly definite way. The theology of Ritschl was historically a reaction against the speculative tendency of German theology at the end of the Eighteenth and the beginning of the Nineteenth Centuries. Schleiermacher, who may be regarded as the founder of modern German theology, was a philosopher as well as a theologian. Baur, the founder of the Tübingen School, was a disciple of Hegel. These men had no objection to Christian dogma; only they interpreted it in the light of the Hegelian philosophy. For Christian doctrine so interpreted they cared more than for the historical Christ. The tendency was to turn Christianity into a speculative philosophy. To Ritschl and his followers dogma and philosophy were very little; the historical Christ was everything. They turned aside from the traditional dogma, not because (as others would have said) it was based upon an obsolete metaphysic, but just because it was metaphysic. They tended to base the evidence of Christianity—sometimes it would appear even the belief in God—upon the impression produced upon the individual soul by the contemplation of Christ's historical personality. That contemplation carries with it an immediate assurance that in Him God is revealed; and that revelation carries with it life and health to the individual soul. The results of criticism are fully accepted, but it is asserted that the main facts about Christ's life and teaching are beyond reasonable question. Questions about miracles, whether the miraculous is accepted or denied, are treated as of little or no importance. The Divinity of Christ may be accepted in a general way, but no value is attached to the dogmatic formulae of the Creeds or the Councils or the dogmatic theologians. Harnack—the best known of living Ritschlians—will go as far as to say (with St. Paul) that God

99

was in Christ reconciling the world to Himself, but
he has no use for further definitions. Even the development of doctrine which is found in the New
Testament itself is treated as of little importance, in
spite of a disposition, common to all Lutheran theology, orthodox and unorthodox alike, to find the
essence of Christianity in St. Paul and in Luther.
St. Paul's idea of justification by faith is interpreted
in such a way as to make it express much the same
thing as their own conception of a revelation of God
through Christ and Christ only. Philosophical arguments for Christianity, the approximations to Christianity in other religions (even the Jewish), the de-
velopments of Christianity since Christ, are all alike
depreciated. The principle of development, whether
in doctrine, in worship, in ethics, or in Church organisation, is rejected. Everything that was added to the
teaching of Christ is regarded as of little or no value
—at least down to the Reformation, which is usually
treated (with some defiance of history) as a return to
the earliest and simplest Christianity. Ritschl himself was disposed to make much of the Church, though
rather in the old Lutheran manner—simply as the
means whereby the preaching of the Word reaches the
individual soul. Disparagement of the Church and
its worship is more decidedly a note of such modern
Ritschlianism as Harnack's. It is hardly too much
to say (with Dr. Sanday) that Harnack seldom if
ever uses the words dogma, Church, worship, without
a note of disparagement. The best of the Ritschlians
are by no means what some people would call mere in-
tellectualists; on the contrary, their tendency is to disparage what the intellect has got to say against Faith
as well as what it can do to support Faith. Moreover,
some of the Ritschlians are men of very great personal
piety; but their religion is of a strictly personal kind.
It rests upon a personal conviction, a personal acceptance of Christ, which is almost independent alike of
the organised Christian society and of intellectual

defences. Perhaps I can best express the tendency of the Ritschlian School by saying that (if we make allowance for certain differences between continental Protestantism and all English Protestantism) it represents an Evangelicalism which has accepted Criticism and which has abandoned a rigorous insistence upon the Protestant dogmatics.

The Catholic Modernists have taken over from Liberal Protestantism the historical and critical treatment of the Bible, of ecclesiastical history, of dogma itself. But, both as a consequence of the religious bent which they have derived from Catholicism and with the more or less unconscious design of rendering their position as acceptable as possible to Catholics, they seek to differentiate their position as widely as possible from that of Liberal Protestantism. So far from resting their faith almost entirely upon the *ipsissima verba* of Christ Himself, they tend rather to disparage the permanent value and importance of Christ's own words, or at all events to insist very strongly upon their need of development. Accepting the most extreme view of the eschatological character of Christ's own thoughts and teaching, regarding as genuine all those sayings (which used often to be doubted or explained away by Liberals) which seem to imply that Christ expected a catastrophic coming again in the very near future, they emphasise the difference between His intellectual outlook and that of the modern world. They complain that the Liberals have so interpreted Christ's own religious and moral teaching as to make of Him a Western, a modern, a Liberal Protestant. So far from depreciating the Church, Loisy declares that the greatest thing Christ ever did was to found the Church. While acknowledging that the Church got its first inspiration and the germs of all the truth which it represents from Christ, it is hardly too much to say that to the Modernist the Church is more than the personal Christ. Unlike the Ritschlians, they recognise the necessity for development in doctrine, in worship, in ecclesiastical organisation. They recognise that the doctrine of the Church is not actually to be found in the teaching of Christ Himself, much of it not anywhere in the New Testament; but they contend that it is an indispensable part of the Church's function to bring out ever more and more what is eternal in the teaching of its Founder, to apply it to the needs and the circumstances of successive ages, to adapt it to the growing knowledge and experience of the world in other departments of life. While they are able in this way to vindicate the necessity of dogma and to justify the formal acceptance of it on the part of the individual priest or layman, they are able at the same time to deny its claims to absolute or final truth and invariability. The Church must still continue her work of constant reinterpretation, application, development.

With regard to metaphysical truth, this attitude is intelligible enough. But the historical statements included in Christian doctrine are more difficult to treat in this spirit. The Modernist way of dealing with statements of history in the Christian creed, so far as their historical character is doubted, is to emphasise the distinction between religion and theology, between truths of faith and truths of reason; statements, such as the Virgin Birth or the bodily Resurrection, which may not be true of the historical Christ may be true in their application to the Christ of faith. Another expedient of the Modernist is to turn away from the metaphysical interpretation and to understand it as merely enjoining a certain practical attitude. M. le Roy, the lay philosopher of the movement, tries to find a defence even for the more recently invented dogmas of the Roman Church by putting them into a practical form. The doctrine of Transubstantiation means that we ought to treat the Eucharist with as much reverence as if Christ were actually present. The Infallibility of the Pope means that the Pope ought to be obeyed as if he were infallible, and so on.

There are few of us who have not to apply to some part of our own traditional formularies some kind or other of liberalising interpretation. And of course a Roman Catholic, touched at all by the modern spirit, has to apply it more extensively, because he has more and more unhistorical dogmas to defend, and he is allowed less liberty in saying what he really thinks about them. But it must not be supposed that these devices— strongly reminiscent of the mode of interpreting the XXXIX Articles advocated by the *Tracts for the Times*—were mere means of getting over difficulties of what we should call Subscription (though a Roman priest is not actually asked to subscribe anything at his Ordination). The divergence of the Catholic Modernist from the German Liberal Protestantism is due to the fact that most of these men were not merely passionately Christian in sentiment, but were also in a very real sense Catholics who desired to remain such. The leader of the movement, M. Loisy, has, unfortunately, since his condemnation, broken with the Church altogether, and avowed a position which he himself hardly regards as Christianity at all. But there were others whose attachment not merely to the Christian Church in a wider sense, but to the Roman Church as it actually is, was much more profound. Whatever may be thought of Loisy, no reader of Tyrrell's *Life* can doubt that he was a man of a profoundly religious nature. The idea of the Catholic Church, the actual worship and practices of the Roman Communion, were the very breath of his life. He clung to that Church long after he had parted with all belief in any distinctively Roman or Catholic doctrine, and had adopted an intellectual attitude which even from the point of view of German Protestantism would have been regarded as amounting to the extremist Liberalism. When he was suspended, he felt his inability to say Mass as an almost physical privation; he describes himself as suffering from " altar-hunger." And so while he might easily have joined the Church of England or (if that were not comprehensive enough for him) some other denomination, he deliberately refused to do so, and preferred to die an excommunicated Roman to deserting by any act of his own the Church which exercised upon him so irresistible a fascination.

This attitude of even the extremer Modernists—men who have quite consciously given up any belief in the exclusive claims of the Roman branch of the Church—powerfully illustrates the fact that, in spite of their agreement with the intellectual position of Liberal Protestantism, there is a profound difference of religious attitude between the Modernist Roman and the typical German Liberal. If this is so even with the extremer Modernist, it is obviously still more so with the more moderate section. It must be remembered once more that, from the point of view of the Vatican, everyone is a Modernist who does not accept the infallibility of Scripture as defined in the Encyclical *Providentissimus Deus*. To deny the Mosaic authorship of the Pentateuch, to deny the story of Noah's ark or the sun standing still, to hold that the Epistle to the Hebrews was not written by St. Paul, to deny that the text about the three heavenly witnesses is part of the genuine text of St. John's First Epistle—to hold these or any other of the most universally accepted conclusions of modern scholarship is Modernism. From the Roman point of view the Bishop of Oxford[1] would be treated as almost as far gone in Modernism as the Bishop of Hereford.[2] M. Batiffol was removed from the Rectorship of the Catholic Institute at Toulouse for adopting very much the position of Bishop Gore, and expressing it with more reserve than he has done.

What are we to think of the Modernist movement? You will not expect me to discuss all, or indeed any, of the particular questions about which the Modernists

[1] Then Dr. Charles Gore.—EDD.
[2] Then Dr. Hensley Henson.—EDD.

are at issue with their enemies—the party who are best described as Traditionalists. About many of them, the Modernists differ among themselves as much as they differ from their opponents. To my own mind there is much which is unsatisfactory about the actual theology of the Modernists. Their Theism in some cases is not always as clear and definite as I could wish. They either have no philosophical basis for it, or they incline to sceptical philosophies more or less connected with the phase of thought known as Pragmatism—a phase of thought with which I personally have no sympathy and which I believe to supply a most precarious basis for a theology of any kind. Their Theism sometimes borders on Pantheism; when that is not so, it seems to me to rest too much upon what they call subjective religious experience or faith. Men who have revolted from Scholasticism are apt to distrust all systems of Metaphysical or Natural Religion. And when they come to discuss the actual content of Christian doctrine, the necessity they are under of formally accepting the whole mass of Roman dogmas drives them to somewhat sophistical shifts. They have got to construct some sort of philosophical defence or explanation not merely for the Incarnation and the Atonement but for Transubstantiation, the Immaculate Conception, the Infallibility of the Pope. The attempt to represent that things are true for faith which are not true for reason or for history is unsatisfactory. Nevertheless we have a great deal to learn from the Modernists. Their criticism of German Liberal Protestantism seems to me largely justified. Although in some quarters this criticism has been unwisely seized upon as a new weapon of offence against Protestantism in general, the Modernists have put the essential principles of Theological Liberalism in a way which is likely to appeal to many English Churchmen much more than the extremely individualistic view of Religion presented by men like Harnack and

Hermann. The influence of their teaching has been widely felt in our Church, especially among the younger clergy. Men who were not interested in Criticism so long as it was supposed that it was an article made in Germany, and imported into this country by Scotch Presbyterians, Nonconformists, and University dons of quite uncatholic proclivities, began to think there might really be something in it when it was taught by men who spoke French and wore chasubles. But the grounds of the attraction which it has exercised over such men are much deeper than that. The Modernists understand the idea of the Church—and consequently one most important aspect of Christianity—in a way that a German Lutheran can never understand it. (I say a German Lutheran, for it would not be true to say that of all Protestants.) German Liberal Protestants are often really religious men; but they are not as a rule very devotional. German services are dull and uninteresting; and the Lutheran can seldom get over the prejudice that to attach any serious importance to external rites is superstitious and Catholic. Such words as ritual or ceremonial are positively abhorrent to him. His conception of the Church is simply that it is the society for public worship, and he is apt to depreciate public worship. He has little appreciation of the idea of an organised Christian community: religion is to him a quite private affair between God and the soul. Moreover, the Modernists take a far more philosophical view of Christianity and its relation to other religions than is common among German Liberals—at least of the Ritschlian variety. They recognise the supremacy of the Christian Revelation, but still they see in it a chapter, though it is the most important chapter, in the religious history of the world; like the old Greek Fathers, they do not think it necessary to deny or disparage the approximation to Christianity which may be found in Judaism, in the Oriental religions, in Plato, or in the Stoics. Still

106

more emphatically the Modernists are right in maintaining the necessity for development in doctrine, in
ethics, in Church life and organisation. It is quite
impossible to defend such a doctrine as the Homo-
ousian without admitting this principle. It was absolutely necessary that the new truth of Christianity,
which had sprung up in a Jewish environment, should
be made intelligible to Greeks, and placed in due relation to the highest thought of that age—which was of
course Greek thought. Equally right are they in insisting that this expression of Christianity in the
terms of Greek philosophy is not necessarily final. It
wants translation into the language of our age, and
the development must be carried further. Our view
of the universe is wholly different from that of the
first Christian ages: it is obviously necessary that our
thoughts about God and about Christ should be in large
measure reconstructed also in view of that difference.
But sometimes the insistence upon the Church, the
sacraments, the necessity of development, leads to an
under-estimate of the personal Christ and His influence. We can get more help towards understanding and appreciating Christ Himself, His teaching,
the importance of personal attachment to Him, from
the best of the Ritschlians—and, I may add, other
Liberal Protestants, German, French, English—than
we can from the Modernists. The best Liberal Protestants have a better appreciation of the historical
Christ and the importance of believing in Him; on
the other hand, the Modernists appreciate much better
that equally important article of the Christian Creed
—" I believe in the Holy Spirit; the Lord and Giver
of life, who spake (and still speaks) by the Prophets."
I believe we may learn from both of these schools.
And I believe that we in the English Church, if we
take to facing theological problems as honestly and
thoroughly as has been done by both of the continental
schools, will be able to combine what is true in both
ways of thinking, and avoid the errors and exag-

gerations of either. We shall make more of the Church (both in idea and in practice) than the Liberal Protestant, without substituting the Church for the personal Christ. We may recognise the value and inevitability of development without our theology ceasing to be as intensely Christo-centric as it is with the best Germans. We may recognise the necessity of much development—much building upon the one foundation—building of very different values, wood, straw, and stubble as well as gold and silver, while we cling to the principle that Christ is the one foundation. And this foundation must be the historical Christ—not a Christ of faith interpreted to mean a Christ who is purely ideal and imaginary.

I have said enough about the differences between the Liberal Protestant and the Catholic Modernist types of Liberalism. And now I should like to emphasise the one point on what they are essentially agreed. They both agree in accepting the principle that there must be a free and thorough-going criticism of the Scriptures, of traditional doctrine, of traditional notions of ecclesiastical history. Of course there is no complete agreement in results. But the most important effect of a loyal and fearless application of critical principles is not so much particular results as the general attitude of mind which is produced by the real facing of difficulties and in particular by the acceptance of the historical mode of investigating Christian doctrine. The most important result of serious study of modern critical theology is that it tends to get rid of the assumption which among ourselves is apt to be made at every turn in the debates of Convocation, at clerical meetings, in the religious newspapers—the assumption that everything has been settled once for all—that there is a certain body of Christian truth which has been always taught from the first and taught universally, and that we can dispose of a doubt as to some matter of historical fact, of doctrine, or of ethics by saying that

108

there is a *consensus patrum* against it or even by quoting the words of an individual Father. That assumption of an unvarying and universally accepted body of truth cannot outlive serious study. What is now considered orthodox Christian doctrine is the result of a slow evolution; and we cannot suppose that that evolution has definitely stopped in the Fourth or the Sixteenth or the Nineteenth Century. I cannot exaggerate the importance of a changed attitude in this matter on the part of the clergy as a body. The lay world is often not well informed about theological matters in detail. Men quite learned in other directions are often childishly ignorant of elementary matters of fact in this region, whether their ignorance takes the form of wholesale acceptance or wholesale denial. But the great mass of intelligent laymen (especially younger laymen) of a little education—whether it be the academical education of the Oxford first-classman or the self-education of the labour-leader—have at least given up blind reliance upon tradition. They may know little of Criticism in detail. But they do vaguely realise that the enormous changes in our knowledge of the physical universe, of the way the Bible and other ancient literatures were written, of the evolution of other religions, make impossible for us much which was possible for our fathers. And they will not be influenced by a Church whose clergy have nothing to say to them but " this doctrine was condemned at such and such a Council," or " that has always been taught "—even when the statement is true; and frequently it is not. If those who are trying to distinguish between the true and the false in the traditions of the past, to get to the historical facts about the origin of Christianity, to reinterpret or reconstruct Christian doctrine in a way which is intelligible to the modern world, are dealt with as the Modernists have been dealt with by the Roman Curia, our Church will lose all influence over the world. For a moment there was a hope that the French

Church was going to effect a reconciliation between itself and the modern educated world. Those hopes have now been shattered. Since the suppression of Modernism, the Church has ceased to count as an intellectual force in France. And a Church which does not influence the intellect of its age soon ceases to have any influence at all. The fate of the French Church supplies a warning which I hope we shall heed before it is too late.

The acceptance of what is called in the narrower sense Biblical Criticism is only a small part of what is implied in the modern, which means practically the open-minded, attitude towards Religion. But I should like to add a word as to the importance of studying, and studying first-hand, critical works upon the Old and New Testaments. What we are in danger of in the Church of England seems to me not so much actual rejection of Criticism as not taking it seriously enough, of indulging our national habit of illogical compromise, so valuable in the political sphere, in another sphere in which it is not equally satisfactory. No doubt in a sense—in the sense of the Roman Curia—we in the Church of England are nearly all Modernists now. The doctrine of Biblical Infallibility is dead. The most extreme of our Conservatives with any pretension to learning is the Dean of Canterbury. And even he will only say, "The Bible is substantially true from cover to cover," and the adverb would be enough to modernise him in the eyes of the Roman Inquisition. There is all the difference in the world between "almost" and "quite." "Doubt one point, and all is doubtful," the old-fashioned theologian would have said, and that is what the Vatican says now. Dr. Wace is a very old man: among younger men the reservation would generally be carried much further. In fact among the youngest men—however "Catholic," however orthodox in other respects—there is little objection to Criticism as regards the Old Testament. Most of them

probably follow the Bishop of Oxford in practically
dismissing the Old Testament miracles *en bloc*. What
one has chiefly to complain of in the younger men is
rather neglect to study the Old Testament sufficiently to
appreciate the value of its positive teaching, both for
its own sake and for the sake of the light which it
throws upon the New Testament, and to be unduly
reticent on the subject in their pulpits and other teaching. But when we come to the New Testament the
case is different. There is often a willingness to accept the principle of the Higher Criticism in the
abstract. Many a clergyman, for instance, will go
so far as to admit in words the usually accepted theory
as to the origin of the Synoptic Gospels; but having
respectfully made his bow to Criticism, he is apt to
go on his way rejoicing, and entirely to ignore
any positive result of Criticism—to use and
interpret the New Testament just as if Criticism
had thrown no light whatever upon the degree
of certainty which we can attach to the different
strata of the narrative, the different events and the
different sayings of our Lord recorded in the New
Testament. I will give two illustrations of what I
mean. No scholarly person who has seriously given
his mind to the subject will deny that, whoever wrote
the Fourth Gospel, the discourses of our Lord recorded therein cannot be relied upon as records of
Christ's own teaching with the same confidence which
we can feel as to the bulk of the Synoptic sayings.
That is universally admitted by scholarly defenders
of the Johannine authorship. Yet nothing is more
common than to hear those sayings quoted, not merely
in popular preaching but in serious argument by professed theologians, as if they were the *ipsissima verba*
of our Lord. Then again, when we turn to the
Synoptists, there is no better established result of
Criticism than this—that sayings or incidents recorded
in the first Gospel alone (except perhaps the parables)
are (to say the least of it) the most doubtful stratum

of the Synoptic Gospels—a stratum which some quite conservative critics would say cannot be traced back to a period before the early Second Century. Yet nothing is commoner than to hear the sayings about the Church—the sayings about binding and loosing, the tradition of the keys to St. Peter, the command to refer quarrels to the arbitrament of the Church (all of them found in that one Gospel only)—treated as if they were the sufficient and absolutely irrefragable foundation for the most tremendous claims on the part of the Church or the clergy.

And now I almost hear someone saying, "If we once go in for Criticism, if we push Criticism into the region of the Gospel history, will not the result be to produce doubt and uncertainty about everything?" I might answer by asking whether after all it is not our duty to follow truth wherever it leads: if everything in the Gospel history were uncertain, would it not be our duty to know and admit it? At all events, is it not our duty to ascertain whether this is so or not? Or I might reply that to a great degree with very large numbers of people the mischief is already done. They are uncertain about everything—in part because they have to so large an extent lost all confidence in the clergy as expert and trustworthy guides in such matters. An acquaintance with Criticism might show them that the difficulties are not nearly so great as they suppose; it could not possibly add to their uncertainty. But I would rather meet the suggestion with a direct negative. The results of Criticism are not all destructive. In the first place I would remind you that on the most important matters of all, Criticism cannot possibly undermine our faith. The Christian ideal of life is present in the New Testament, however it got there. If Conscience tells us that the words of Christ are true, they would be true even if those words were wholly the creation of the Church, and none of them were really uttered by the historical Jesus. And the same may be said of the

Christian idea of God. Whether it was Christ Himself or the Pharisees who first taught that God should be looked upon as the common Father, that assertion will be equally true and equally precious. But it cannot be too emphatically stated that the attempts to deny that Jesus was an historical personality, and that the Synoptic Gospels give us in the main a true historical picture of His character and teaching, have altogether broken down; and it is honest historical Criticism that has broken them down. About this the real experts are practically unanimous. The recent attempts to prove the contrary are not the work of trained and competent theologians or historians, but of amateurs educated in some quite different sphere of work, who have invaded a province which is not their own. And it must always be remembered that, even if we can never be certain that any one particular saying of Jesus is quite correctly reported, that does not throw any uncertainty upon the general character of His teaching; for the doubtful saying, when it is not inconsistent with the general tenor of Christ's teaching, owes its existence to the impression produced by the rest.

But it will be said, " At all events, Criticism throws doubt upon the miraculous elements in the life of Christ." I have said nothing about this question, because to have dealt with it at all adequately would have occupied the whole of my time. But I do not like to seem to have shirked the subject altogether, and I will therefore conclude with one word on the subject. In the first place, it must be remembered that many so-called miracles may not be really violations of the laws of nature at all; many unusual or abnormal events in the Gospel history may quite conceivably have happened, and yet not be violations of natural laws. Much present-day thought and discovery encourage the belief in the influence of mind over matter of a kind which may be described as abnormal, and which would be popularly set down as miraculous. Few sober critics of the present day would be prepared to treat the narratives of Christ's spiritual healings as purely mythical or legendary in the summary fashion which was at one time common among sceptical critics. Few perhaps will dispute the strong evidence for the actual occurrence of visions of the Risen Lord, apart from any theory as to their nature. Nor must it be assumed that Criticism will *necessarily* compel us to give up those events which, if true, can hardly be regarded otherwise than as miracles in the most uncompromising, old-fashioned sense. As a matter of fact there are competent and honest critics who regard the evidence for the Virgin Birth and the bodily Resurrection (as distinct from visions of the Risen Lord) as sufficient to warrant belief. But I doubt whether any competent critic who has really given his mind to these questions will deny that they are less certain than the non-miraculous events of Christ's life and very much less certain than His best authenticated sayings. It is impossible to read what has been written in defence of the Virgin Birth by such men as the Bishop of Ely [1] without seeing that, though they think the balance of evidence inclines in its favour, they do not deny that the doubts felt about it by other competent critics are altogether unreasonable. They accept the fact, but chiefly because other than purely historical considerations have already prepared them to regard Jesus as an exceptional, a unique personality in whose life-history such exceptional events might be expected. The Incarnation or the Divinity of Christ is not proved by the Virgin Birth; rather it is the Incarnation of Christ which renders the Virgin Birth credible to such men. And from this a further result seems to flow. On these presuppositions the question of the miraculous cannot be regarded as a matter of the very first importance. The Christian Revelation can no longer be treated as resting for its credibility mainly upon

[1] Dr. F. H. Chase.—EDD.

the external guarantee of miracles. And if that is so, our belief in Christian doctrine would not be seriously affected if the progress of Criticism should lead to their general rejection. The knowledge that there is this element of doubt about the miraculous is becoming widely diffused among persons of even very moderate education. And that knowledge is generally sufficient to make it impossible for them to accept a presentation of Christianity which assumes that its truth stands or falls with the historical evidence for miracles. They may not deny the miracles, they may be inclined to accept them; but they feel that they have not the knowledge or the leisure to examine the question for themselves. They feel that the real grounds of their faith must be sought elsewhere. If the more general study of critical methods and results should lead the clergy to adopt a type of preaching and teaching which does not seem to make Christian belief synonymous with belief in the suspension of natural law, that would to my mind be a very desirable result. Many different attitudes of mind on this subject are quite consistent with honest acceptance and application of critical methods. Serious study may lead to acceptance of the miraculous—acceptance of the kind which we reasonably accord to truths which rest on a certain degree of probable evidence. It may lead to rejection in the sense in which we may be said to reject alleged events which seem to us inadequately proved or improbable. It may lead to suspension of judgement, with or without a leaning to the one side or the other. All these are possible and reasonable attitudes, all these represent conclusions at which honest men acquainted with the facts do actually arrive. But, whatever attitude is accepted by individual thinkers on this matter, nothing, I believe, can be asserted with more certainty than this—that the world will be less and less disposed to accept a religion which is supposed to rest wholly or mainly upon the evidence of miracle. The ultimate ground for the acceptance of Christianity must be found in the appeal which is made to Reason and Conscience by the truths which it asserts, and upon the impressions made upon the soul by the life and teaching and personality of its Founder. If Criticism leads to increased emphasis upon deeper grounds for Christian belief than is supplied by miracles, its influence will not be destructive. Whether the miracles are accepted or rejected, no faith is worth much which rests primarily upon miracles. For no man can say that Jesus is Lord but by the Holy Spirit.

VII

THE LIFE OF NEWMAN [1]

THERE is hardly any personality in the religious history of the Nineteenth Century who is so well known to most English Churchmen—nay, to all Englishmen who take any interest in ecclesiastical movements—as John Henry Newman. His own autobiography has become a classic, and a whole literature has sprung up about him and the movement in which he was the central figure. But the Newman that we know was Newman the Anglican—the man who at the age of forty-five, after initiating a movement which revolutionised, for good or for evil, the Anglican Church—left that Church to become a Roman Catholic priest. Most of us have read the *Apologia*; we know a few other of the books which he wrote since he became a Roman, especially the *Idea of a University*. We know—especially since the revelations in the life of Manning—that he was long suspected and neglected by the authorities of his adopted Church, and that in his old age he became a Cardinal, under the comparatively liberal pontificate of Leo XIII. But as to what he did with himself during the greater part of his retired life at Edgbaston, and as to why we did not hear more of him, most of us know little enough. The veil has now been lifted by the publication of Mr. Wilfrid Ward's fascinatingly interesting book.

It would have been well perhaps for the reputation of the Church which he joined and to which he adhered at such a cost if that veil had not been drawn. In the conversion of Newman, the Roman Church made the greatest conquest that its modern annals have to record. It had conquered the most famous religious personality which had appeared during the Nineteenth Century in what (if we allow for the fact that half Germany is Catholic) may be called the

[1] *The Life of John Henry Cardinal Newman*, 2 vols. By Wilfrid Ward. (London, 1912.) Reprinted from *The Modern Churchman*, vol. ii (1912–13), pp. 33–45.

leading Protestant nation, and the Protestant nation on which religion had retained its strongest hold—the most distinguished ornament of one of the two great English Universities, a master of the English tongue, the leader of a party which was already well on its way to secure that dominant position in the English Church which it has since acquired. And he did not go alone: he was accompanied by a band of men who, though (with very few exceptions) on quite a different intellectual plane from himself, were clergymen much above the average in learning, ability, and powers of influence, together with a good handful of not unimportant laymen.

If Newman had done all this for the Church of Rome by his teaching in the Anglican Church and by the mere act of leaving it, what might he not be expected to do for it as one of its accredited ministers! And yet, what use did that Church actually make of him? A sadder record of a comparatively wasted life—whether we look upon it from our own point of view or from that of his Church—could hardly be imagined. It seems as if everybody in the Roman Church had deliberately set himself to reduce Newman to insignificance, to thwart all that he attempted, to amuse him with tasks which would keep him quiet but which could lead to no result of importance. They were eager enough to exploit his Anglican reputation, but his name (as he sometimes complains himself) was about all they wanted of him.

For a moment, indeed, he was welcomed and made much of. He was allowed to choose his own sphere of work; he chose to be an Oratorian, and settled himself down as the Superior of a little band of Oxford converts in the neighbourhood of Birmingham. Then they made him Rector of the new Catholic University in Ireland. The whole scheme was ill-considered. It sprang rather from a desire to keep men out of the " mixed " Queen's Colleges than

THE LIFE OF NEWMAN

from any desire to secure a true University for
Catholics. For a few years Newman was snubbed,
neglected, hampered, by the Irish Bishops. A real
University—the true meaning of which, in spite of
all his theological limitations, Newman understood
so well and expounded so eloquently—was the last
thing the Irish Bishops really wanted; what they
wanted was a lay Seminary, managed by themselves,
with Newman as the submissive agent of their domi-
nation. So jealous were they of his lay influence that
he could not even get the accounts put into the hands
of a competent layman. The only thing that can be
said for them is that the notion that one man could
effectively combine the headship of a University at
Dublin with the superiorship of a religious house at
Birmingham was from the first an impossible one,
and Newman hardly showed the great practical wisdom and sagacity which he usually displayed in thinking otherwise. Then they set him to prepare a re-
vised English translation of the Bible for Catholics.
He obeyed, though without much enthusiasm. The
task was one for which he possessed absolutely no
qualifications, except the one so conspicuously lacking
to our own New Testament revisers—a mastery of
the English tongue. He does not appear to have been
a Hebrew scholar, and had never made a study of
the New Testament; he did not, indeed—any more
than any other of the movement's leaders—know
what real study of the New Testament meant.

After working for several years upon it, he found
that the English Bishops took no interest in the
scheme: it is not clear that they had any intention
of adopting the translation if he ever finished it. Then
he was pressed to edit a Catholic periodical, *The Rambler.* " A bitter penance," he called it, and it was
made a penance to him. He was incessantly abused
for the too liberal tone of some of his contributors
which he did his best to restrain; eventually delated
to Rome for venturing, in an article " on consulting

the faithful in matters of doctrine," to suggest that there was a period when the Church had not ideally performed the functions of the *Ecclesia Docens*; and was finally called upon to resign the editorship. He obeyed the order with the same meekness which he had shown in suspending the *Tracts for the Times* at the behest of his Anglican Bishop.

Then came the saddest part of his life. He was getting old. He knew that his proper task was writing—attempting to meet the religious difficulties of his age, not merely the difficulties of Protestants and Anglicans as against Romanism, but the more fundamental difficulties in the way of Christian Theism and Christianity in general. Yet he felt himself so much surrounded by an atmosphere of suspicion, jealousy, and slander, that it was simply impossible for him to write. He dreaded above all things the slightest aspersion on his orthodoxy—even the milder weapons in his Church's well-equipped arsenal of anathema, an episcopal censure, a book placed on the Index, a reported word of disapproval by the Pope or the Prefect of the Propaganda. And he knew that he could not express himself fully—that is to say, he could not depart from the mere repetition of accepted theological commonplaces—without exposing himself to these things or worse. He deliberately condemned himself to silence, devoted himself to the routine duties of the Oratory Church at Birmingham, and to the management of the school which he had started there, though he did not apparently (except in emergencies) take much part in the teaching. The Oratory School was the only one of his undertakings which can be said to have prospered at all. Even this was somewhat actively discouraged, and at one time he had great difficulty in preventing it being suppressed on the ground that the preparation which it afforded for Oxford was encouraging the reprobated and all but forbidden " mixed education."

All this time, during which Newman was " under

---

a cloud " at Rome and among his own co-religionists, he was equally unpopular among Protestants. For the public in general he was " not dead but buried." It will seem perfectly amazing, now that it has been agreed that Newman is to be treated as an English classic—as an exception to the negligibility of most sermon writers and all Roman theologians—to learn that between 1848 and 1864 he was unable to get books published except at his own expense, and that he lost money over what he did publish. Kingsley's blundering attack upon the veracity of himself and other Catholics gave him an opportunity of emerging from his obscurity. The *Apologia* appeared in weekly parts in 1864. He wrote it from hand to mouth under extreme pressure—at one time spending twenty-two consecutive hours in writing! It took the world by storm: thenceforth Newman became a personality again for the British public. But it did not at once dispel the " cloud." He actually had to send a special embassy to Rome to clear away the mists of suspicion which still hung about his name at the Vatican and the Propaganda, and to contradict a few of the slanders which Manning's allies had kept in circulation about him. One of these people naïvely explained to him that if a man in his position wanted to keep in favour with the authorities he must maintain (as Manning did) a perpetual correspondence with agents at Rome, and even come to Rome himself periodically.

> " I ought (he told me) to send persons to Rome from time to time to explain things and keep authorities at Rome *au courant*. I ought to go to Rome myself." [1]

Nobody's reputation was safe at Rome unless he took special steps to defend it.

The last of Newman's disappointments was his failure to get leave to establish himself in Oxford—nominally as the ordinary Priest of the " Oxford

[1] II, 189.

Mission," really with a view to influencing Catholic
and other undergraduates.   He was allowed to spend
some thousands of pounds (his own and his friends')
upon buying land in Oxford, and to go on collecting
money to build a church after the Bishop of Birmingham had received secret instructions that, if he attempted to establish himself at Oxford, he was *blande
sauviterque* to prevent him.   Newman's appointment
as a consulting theologian to the Vatican Council
showed that at last he had convinced the authorities
of his orthodoxy.   And finally, under Leo XIII, when
he was too old to do much good or much harm,
honours and recognition were showered upon him,
and Catholics who believed that—within, however,
strict limits—thought and learning and independence
were not altogether out of place within the pale of
the Roman Church, even in a priest, began to think
that a better time was coming.   What has become of
those hopes, we all know.

What was the cause of all this suspicion and hosti-
lity?   Many will be disposed to answer: " Newman
was too liberal for them."   The answer is true, if a
man can be " too liberal " without being liberal at all.
Readers of the *Apologia* know very well that opposition to Liberalism—in politics and theology—was the
ruling principle of Newman's early life.   An abject
dread of " the Revolution " and the liberty of thought
which " the Revolution " brought with it started " the
Oxford Movement."   Newman's horizon did somewhat widen when he found himself a progressive in
a world of reactionaries, instead of a reactionary in
a world that was beginning to move; but all the same
a thorough-going opponent of Liberalism he remained
to the end of his days.   People are very unwilling
to admit that a man of brilliant intellectual gifts can
really believe what seems to them absurd.   Especially
since the Modernists have found it convenient to make
use of his doctrine of Development, Newman is often
set down as a " liberal Catholic " or even a

"Modernist." Nothing can be further from the truth. Newman's mind was naturally prone to superstition. Instances are recorded of this tendency in childhood. After he became a Roman, he indulged in devotions to the Virgin which sober Catholics of perfect orthodoxy condemned. He believed things at which highly-educated priests are apt to smile—the liquefaction of the blood of St. Januarius, for instance. His way of talking about the saints is really quite pagan in its naïveté. When he was being prosecuted for libel by the infamous ex-friar Achilli, he writes (it is fair to remember that he is writing to nuns):

> "I went on saying to the last moment, 'I will not believe, till I see it, that Our Lady and St. Philip will suffer it.' . . . Mary is taking the best way, depend upon it, for our victory." "I am not certain that I shall not be obliged even yet to confess that your Madonna has got me off." [1]

He held a "novena" to St. Anthony for the discovery of sufficient witnesses. He seriously thinks it will be a special advantage to him that

> "our House in Birmingham is erected under the Invocation of the Immaculate Mother of God." [2]

A man who had only God to trust to would be in a poor way, one is left to conclude. And Mary, it appears, interferes with the administration of justice only when she has been flattered. No doubt this tendency to revel in things which would shock Protestant minds is specially characteristic of the first fresh fervour of the convert. In particular, his belief in the Pope personally as always guided by the Holy Spirit even in his non-infallible utterances and actions wore off to some extent with further experi-

---

[1] Vol. I, 293, 294.　　　　[2] Vol. I, 288, 289.

ence of the actual Pontiff and the wretched crew by
which he was surrounded. But he was as far as
ever from being a liberal. He had, indeed, a wholesome respect for the claims of Science and for the
claims of History—the only branch of knowledge in
which he was really learned, though even there his
learning was not of the critical type. In later years
he even divined that Criticism was a thing that had
to be reckoned with, though he apparently knew very
little of what it really meant. But with all the amazing limitations of his knowledge and of his mind—
which were just the limitations of Oxford education
and Anglican Theology in the thirties—he was after
all (to use the modern slang) an "intellectual." He
had a respect for the claims of reason, of knowledge,
of truth. He wanted to think, to grapple with problems honestly, to say what he thought, to be fair to
opponents. Though he knew little of Philosophy in
the technical sense, he had a philosophical mind—a
tendency to theorise, and great dialectical power in
defending a theory. And all this was what average
Catholics could not forgive. They rightly felt in a
vague way that he did not belong to them. He could
not help constantly betraying, in the favourite phrase
of Catholic detraction, a "want of Catholic instinct."
Prostrate himself before authority as abjectly as he
might, he demanded a reason for his submission: he
recognised that there were limits to it. He had a
capacity for criticising men and things which, with all
his submissiveness, could not altogether be suppressed.
He could not stoop to the petty intrigues by which
men like Manning made their way into favour and
into power. In particular, he would not abuse and
disparage the Church of England, Oxford, everything
else outside "the Church," as heartily as was expected. He could not compass sea and land to make
one proselyte; he could not help regarding the defence
of fundamental beliefs for the benefit of the English-
speaking world as a matter of more importance than

the capture of a few young men of wealth or family for the Roman Church.

Here are two illustrations of the collision between Newman and his environment.

" In reply to a friend who in 1864 spoke of setting on foot an historical Review, he wrote: ' Nothing would be better than a historical Review, but who would bear it? Unless one doctored all one's facts, one would be thought a bad Catholic. The truth is, there is a keen conflict going on just now between two parties, one in the Church and one out of it. And at such seasons extreme views alone are in favour and a man wh⌟ is not extravagant is thought treacherous. I sometimes think of King Lear's daughters and consider that they, after all, may be found the truest who are in speech more measured.' " [1]

The following is from a letter of Lord Acton in reference to the opposition to *The Rambler*:

" I had a three hours' talk with the venerable Newman, who came out with his real sentiments to an extent which startled me with respect both to things and persons, as Ward, Dalgairns, etc., etc.; natural inclination of men in power to tyrannise; ignorance and presumption of would-be theologians. I did not think he would ever cast aside his diplomacy and buttonment so entirely, and was quite surprised at the intense interest he betrayed in *The Rambler*. He was quite miserable when I told him the news, and moaned for a long time, rocking himself backwards and forwards over the fire like an old woman with a tooth-ache. He thinks the move [the denunciation to the authorities of an article by Döllinger] provoked both by the hope of breaking down *The Rambler,* and by jealousy of Döllinger." [2]

[1] Vol. I, 571 f.
[2] Vol. I, 481. [Acton's letter was addressed to Richard Simpson.—EDD.]

To the last Newman always professed to have found religious "peace" in the Roman communion. Personal religious peace he probably did find there, though he was hardly the man to find absolutely unruffled peace in any communion. He had made a great sacrifice in obedience to intellectual conviction, and there is no evidence in these volumes that his conviction ever wavered. The personal effacement and personal chagrin which he experienced in that communion fitted in with his conception of God's dealing with the Church: they were his "cross," and his knowledge of ecclesiastical history always enabled him to console himself with cases in which similar neglect, misunderstanding, and want of appreciation had been the lot of those now acknowledged as Saints and Doctors of the Church. But it is impossible to read these pages without seeing that Newman's experience of the Roman Church from within was a huge disillusionment. Very soon the first enthusiasm of the convert had evaporated, and after that he shows an extraordinarily sane and sober judgement of men and things in his own Church and in others. He recognises fully enough that the moral tone of communities which were within the bosom of the true Church was not higher—often not so high—as that of communities which he was obliged to regard as technically "outside the Church."

And, of course, his ingenious mind was fertile in theories, which accounted for the discrepancy between what might naturally have been supposed to follow from his principles and the actual facts.

"We are in a world of imperfection—truth and its propagation is committed to 'earthen vessels.' Hence some Saints—as St. Basil, St. Jerome, St. Thomas M., St. Joseph Calasanctius, St. Alfonso —have been neglected at Rome during their lifetime." [1]

[1] Vol. I, 483.

So he writes when Döllinger (long before his revolt) had been silenced, and when he was expecting a similar fate for *The Rambler* and its staff. He was ever ready to assert the duty of submitting to " authority," while he had no delusions at all as to the way in which authority was likely to be exercised in practice—the motives which inspired it, the character of the men who pulled the wires to which authority responded as mechanically as the figures in the puppet-show respond to the hand of the showman. The odd thing is that he should have been able still to believe in the special, exclusive supernatural direction of an organism whose very human psychology he so thoroughly understood. He hardly concealed from himself that the Roman Church in this age—even from his own orthodox, conservative, and not at all " modernist " point of view—was a vast organisation for stopping in every direction the progress of knowledge, for checking all serious intellectual activity, and for driving intelligent men into infidelity, agnosticism, and secularism. And he really cared for the progress of knowledge and the activity of intellect—both for their own sake and as a means to the attainment and diffusion of religious truth. And yet he thought it his duty meekly to submit, and to give up serious writing or teaching, lest a word should escape his lips which, reported to an ignorant and quite unspiritual Italian prelate at the other end of Europe by a malicious informer in a garbled extract badly translated, should bring down upon him the dreaded " censure "! It never seems to have occurred to him to revise the premisses which led to so monstrous a conclusion. He could not recognise that such a state of things, owing to the actual constitution of human nature and human society, was the natural and inevitable consequence of a theory which required implicit obedience and at least external submission in matters of Theology, Philosophy, History, and even Church policy to such very " earthen vessels " as Pius IX, or Cardinal Barnabo, or Cardinal Wiseman, or Cardinal Manning.

And it is not only the Roman theory of the Church on which Newman's experiences form such an instructive comment. The ideal of the Church as conceived by High Anglicans is after all much the same as that of the Roman Church; the only difference lies in their views as to where the best realisation of that ideal is to be found. The Roman Church really can boast of all those things the absence of which our higher Anglicans profess to deplore in our own Church—a sense of the supreme importance of " dogmatic truth," a vigilant Episcopate ready to suppress the smallest departure from traditional opinions, a habit of docile submission on the part of the " faithful laity," wherever a faithful laity exists. And yet the development of that High Anglican system has been made possible only because the Church and people of England were in fact so very Protestant that they did not possess, or could not effectively exercise, those methods for the control of opinion which, according to the theory, the Church exists to wield. For those who are unencumbered by any theory of an infallible Pope or an infallible Church or a duty of unlimited submission to ecclesiastical authority, there is much in Newman's view of what the Church should be— of the proper attitude of theologians towards advance in other branches of learning, of the proper functions of the theologian as distinct from those of the ecclesiastic or the collective Episcopate, of the necessity for development in doctrine, for a development of new truth which sometimes involves the abandonment of old doctrines—which is in the highest degree interesting and stimulating. He was not a liberal himself, but his theories constantly lend themselves to a liberal interpretation. It was no accident that he was in a sense the parent of Modernism. It was a development of Newman's doctrine of development which helped the avowed Modernists for

128

a time (and how many concealed Modernists now!) to maintain their position in the Roman Communion, though their developed doctrines have really as little in common with Newman's personal views as the doctrines of the Roman Church have with the New Testament ideas out of which Newman supposed them to have been developed. The religious history of the next fifty years will decide whether Newman will be better remembered as the unconscious and unwilling father of continental Modernism or as the leader of the great reaction in the Church of England.

To many readers the book will be most interesting on account of the light which it throws upon Newman's fascinating personality. Certainly his weak points do come into greater prominence than in the skilful and reserved self-portraiture through which we have chiefly known him hitherto—his extreme sensitiveness, his pre-occupation with himself, his somewhat excessive craving for sympathy and appreciation. And yet these qualities were just those which made him lovable. He won sympathy because he craved so much for sympathy—not to say admiration, personal loyalty, and docile discipleship. And assuredly these were just the qualities that made him suffer so intensely from the treatment which he received in the Roman Church. It is rather curious, however, to find that in the *Historia Calamitatum,* which he so frequently repeats in his letters and memoranda, he seems to think that he had been almost as much snubbed and ill-treated in the Church of England as he was in the Church of Rome; though he was quite conscious of the fact that in the Church of England he had wielded enormous influence, while in the Church of Rome the sphere of his influence was a very small one and that some of his old disciples, Faber and W. G. Ward, were now among those who were his most formidable, if not personally unfriendly, opponents. One might have thought that to have re-

I

volutionised the Church of England, to have been the leader of a great party, the idol of an attached circle of friends and disciples, might have made him indifferent to his third class in the schools, the loss of his tutorship, the jealousy of Hawkins, the censure of " the Heads," the hatred of the Evangelicals. Not to feel the treatment which he received in the Church of Rome would have required a man of iron mould. A more completely, I will not say unselfish, but selfless character than Newman might perhaps have thrown himself more heartily into the little tasks which were all that the jealousy and stupidity of the Roman authorities allowed him, and interested himself more in the people with whom it brought him into contact; but there seems little or nothing to criticise in his actual attitude towards his persecutors and detractors. Throughout the narrative he stands forth as a supremely conscientious and high-minded man. If at times his resentment against the small creatures who worried him seems a little excessive, it is not so much a more forgiving disposition that was lacking as the easy good nature which could have accepted friendly advances or apologies without being deceived as to their real value. He was quite free from petty vanity; he was not without pride. Half his troubles were due to the fact that he could not stoop to the practice of the little arts of conciliation and flattery —still less the meanness and intrigue which carried Manning so far. Perhaps there was a trifle too much of this " proper pride " about him. An excessive self-consciousness was his weak point; his religion was too introspective to allow of his losing the thought of himself in work for individuals or for a cause.

Mr. Ward has performed his task with consummate tact, judgement, and literary skill. Never has a biographer introduced less of himself and his own views or merged himself more completely in his subject. His subject, to a Roman Catholic, is a dangerous one: in such a task a man " *incedit per ignes*

Suppositos cineri doloso." It is scarcely possible that he could have moved more warily or discreetly without injustice to the subject of his biography. He has performed an important service to the cause of historical truth, and doubtless he has served the true interests of his Church and of all that is best and highest within it. Whether this book will be altogether a service to that Church considered simply as a proselytising organisation in competition with other Christian bodies is more doubtful. For any Englishman bitten with Roman-ward tendencies I could not imagine a more effective " dissuasive from Popery." To myself it reads also as a powerful dissuasive from ecclesiasticism of any kind. If it does make one feel how much healthier, more natural, more bracing is the atmosphere even of a more or less Romanising Anglicanism, it is only because it makes one realise how Protestant the adherents of that system really are—how much more Protestant than they know, or wish to be. The Roman Church, as exhibited by Mr. Ward's book, is very much what Lord Halifax would like the Church of England to be, with one exception —that the Roman Church would not tolerate a Lord Halifax. The book from beginning to end is a commentary on the value of that religious liberty—liberty for priests as well as for laymen—of which the High Anglicans have availed themselves so amply, however anxious they may be to deny it to others.

VIII

GEORGE TYRRELL [1]

Mr. Ward's *Life of Newman* presented itself to most of us as a great exposure of the modern Roman Church from within. The present work will also read—to outsiders at all events, and probably to not a few within the pale—as an exposure also, but as an exposure of a very different kind. Newman really belonged to the Roman Church; he was completely in sympathy with the Roman Church as it has been at its best. Taking the Roman Church at its own official estimate of itself, Newman ought to have found himself at home in it. That he did not was due to the folly, short-sightedness, and little-mindedness of the *personnel* which was dominant in the Church of his day in England and at Rome. How far the dominance of such persons was inseparable from the system may be disputed; but there seems no reason in the nature of things why wiser men of quite an orthodox type should not have made much of Newman, given him suitable work to do, and used him in the service of their Church—as indeed was done for a short time under the pontificate of Leo XIII.

With Tyrrell it was otherwise. Considering what he was, it cannot be said that, on Roman premisses, he was treated particularly badly. The wonder of most readers will be rather that he was tolerated for so long, and that the final breach came so late. It is the system and not the *personnel* that is " exposed " by the present *Life*. Tyrrell never really belonged in spirit to the Roman Church—still less was his spirit that of its straitest sect, the Jesuit Order to which he belonged. The strange thing is that he was so long in discovering the fact. When one finds Tyrrell continually complaining of the restraints which were put upon him, the traditionalism, immovability, obscurantism, and the like of his Church and his

[1] *Autobiogaphy and Life of George Tyrrell.* 2 vols. Arranged, with supplement, by M.D. Petre. (London, 1912.) Reprinted from *The Modern Churchman,* vol. ii (1912–13), pp. 504–12.

Order, one wonders why he should ever have expected
to find it otherwise; or one *would* wonder, but for
the fact that few converts belonging to the educated
class ever joined the Roman Church in more complete
and näive ignorance of its history, its traditions, and
its present condition. It was a matter of real aston-
ishment to him to discover that the Jesuit Order was
not the home of enlightenment, open-mindedness,
and tolerance. Of course before the end he realised
that he had no more right for such surprise than
at discovering any other organism to be acting
according to the law of its nature; but even his minute
self-analysis hardly explains exactly when the disillusionment finally came, and why it was so long delayed.
And after all, the disillusionment was never complete.
To the very last he cherished a sentimental affection
for a " Catholicism " which to a Protestant mind
seems to have no further relation to the Catholicism
of history than is implied in a decided taste for the
outward forms of Catholic worship.

The first volume of this work is an autobiography
(extending to 1885) of quite extraordinary interest.
It deserves to rank with the great classical auto-
biographies, and would probably do so if Tyrrell's
career had been of a kind to be permanently interesting to the world in general. Of Miss Petre's
continuation of it no more need be said than that
it could hardly have been done better. The autobiography begins with a minute account of the writer's
early recollections and experiences. We may suppose
that an eye to piquant contrasts may have exaggerated
a little the by no means attractive picture which he
draws of his childhood. According to his own account, he was in his early years absolutely non-
religious, and almost, it would appear, non-moral.
Brought up as an Irish Protestant by a mother of
much character and considerable intelligence, he seems
never to have accepted the religious teaching put
before him sufficiently to have been conscious of any

change when he made up his mind that none of it was true.

" I did not cease to be a believer, but, from a non-believer, I became an unbeliever at about the age of ten." [1]

In spite of his attachment to a widowed mother who had a hard struggle with poverty, and to a head master who took him for nothing, he was idle on system—though possibly weak health may to some extent explain his lack of energy—so much so that his abilities were never discovered at all. He almost escaped any real education beyond a very moderate acquaintance with Latin and a mere smattering of Greek. His first interest in religion arose from his attending (by way of novelty) the service at Grangegorman Church, which was considered in Dublin dangerously ritualistic, though in England both teaching and ritual would have been considered very moderately "high." The influence of that church made him a High Anglican, and the friendship of Dolling carried further and deepened the tendency. But though he speaks of this interest as something very superficial and merely intellectual, it did influence him sufficiently to induce him to give up the society of an undesirable friend who had taught him among other things to steal, and was perhaps something rather deeper than he afterwards imagined. Butler's *Analogy* helped him out of Atheism, though he represents himself as hardly a Theist even when he joined the Roman Church and the Jesuit Order. The transformation was gradually completed and he found himself surrounded by people with whom belief was a matter of course.

The resolution to join the Roman Church was taken under the influence of nothing deeper than a sentimental attraction conceived while attending Roman Catholic services in Dublin, combined with a vague

[1] Vol. I, 68.

feeling that here was the real thing of which High
Anglicanism was but an artificial imitation. An attraction to High Anglicanism or Romanism based
at bottom upon aesthetic attraction is by no means an
unusual phenomenon. The curious feature about
Tyrrell's mental evolution is that such an attraction
resulted in a religion of so deep and so markedly
ethical a character. Another curious feature of his
psychology is that from the first there was never a
question with him that, if he became a Christian, he
would be a priest, and if a Roman Catholic, then a
Roman priest. Fears about his own personal salvation
had no influence upon him at all. He seems to have
cared more for other people's souls than for his own.
In the highest sense no doubt such a state of mind
may be considered the truest way of caring about
one's own soul. But with Tyrrell it was not exactly
pure altruism or unselfishness that inspired this desire,
singularly unselfish, or perhaps rather self-less, as he
was. He was in love (we may say) with the idea
of priesthood; and to the last he seems to have cared
passionately not merely for making other people better,
but for keeping them " practising " Catholics, even
at a time when the link which bound him to the Roman
Church was obviously snapping. He had a peculiarly
high sense of the value for character of religious
practices—more so perhaps than of religious beliefs.
It will probably be found that the permanent value
of his works consists in the help they afford in keeping
up and really utilising the habit of prayer and other
religious ordinances by persons who have given up
many of the traditional beliefs associated with them,
and even in spite of much vagueness in intellectual
outlook.

I spoke of the book as being an " exposure " of
Jesuitism. It is an exposure of a very different kind
from that which will be expected by the ordinary
Protestant controversialist. We hear nothing of dis-
honest tricks, over-subtle diplomacy, unscrupulous

intrigue, and the like. His experiences do little to
give one any high opinion of the keen intelligence,
genius for education, and knowledge of the world
with which the Order is generally credited. If Tyrrell's estimate is to be accepted, the training of a Jesuit
is almost as bad as it could possibly be as a means
to the end supposed to be in view. Putting aside
the exceptional case of the man who joins the Order
late in life, the intending Jesuit has generally been
educated at a Jesuit school, where he has, as far as
possible, been kept in ignorance not merely of this
world but even of physiological facts. It is hard to
believe Father Tyrrell's suggestion that many Jesuits
actually discover these facts when they are approaching thirty and beginning Moral Theology; but at all
events ignorance is the ideal aimed at.

During the two years' novitiate the youth leads
a life of constant spiritual exercises and devotional
reading almost unbroken by study. The effect of
such a training is to foster an exaggerated devotion-
ality which is generally laughed at in the Order itself
as soon as its victims have shaken off the influence
of their novitiate. Then the course of Scholastic
Philosophy; then a period of schoolmastering; then
Scholastic Theology. Scholasticism affected Tyrrell
profoundly. This was his true education. The first
stage of his intellectual emancipation consisted in the
attempt to understand St. Thomas in an enlightened
and to some extent modernised sense, and to champion
him against the dominant Suarez. In spite of the
Papal approbation of St. Thomas, this led to the first
silencing of Tyrrell—his suppression as a teacher of
Philosophy; for in the Order it was generally held
that St. Thomas must really mean Suarez. If St.
Thomas and Suarez did not agree, they must be made
to agree. The general impression which Tyrrell gives
one of the Jesuit training is that it represents a long
career of stupid routine, utterly uninfluenced by and
unadapted to the changes in intellectual outlook which

have taken place in Europe since the beginning of the Seventeenth Century, and utterly uncalculated to qualify men for fighting the Church's battles in a world which has so changed.

As to the Jesuits themselves, so far from being men of heroic mould carefully selected on account of their fitness for the highest intellectual gladiatorship, they would seem to be, according to Tyrrell's account, for the most part very ordinary men, intellectually and morally, who have drifted into the career chiefly because to an average boy in the Jesuit School— particularly if he is a " Church-boy," supported by the diocese—it seems to be the easiest thing to do; while the efforts made by its abler members to bring the ideas and the practice of the Order into somewhat greater harmony with the requirements of the modern world seems to be for the most part frustrated by the opposing mass of unintelligent, obstinate tradition- alism. One great misfortune of the Jesuit Order is that it is in the main governed by old men. That misfortune is shared by most other ecclesiastical insti- tutions, but then the rule of Jesuit authorities is more despotic and less amenable to public opinion than that of (say) Anglican Bishops or the Scottish General Assembly. Such are the impressions of Jesuitry which the reader will probably derive from these volumes. How far they are correct, I do not venture to judge.

The reader of these volumes is enabled to trace with considerable minuteness the process of Tyrrell's intellectual emancipation. I will not attempt to sum- marise it. The early stages were due mainly to the spontaneous workings of a naturally alert intelligence on the basis of such materials as the extremely narrow curriculum presented to him. Most influential among his educators was, as has been said, St. Thomas, who was treated by Tyrrell as a thinker and not merely as an authority to be learned by heart. Then there was a middle period in which he came under the influence of Newman, and attempted to bridge over the gulf between the old and the new views of the universe by an extension of Newman's development theory. But the most decisive turning-point in his intellectual growth was constituted by his first acquaintance with recent German Theology under the guidance of Baron von Hügel. From this time the scales fell from his eyes, and he became definitely a Modernist, and eventually a Modernist of the Modernists—almost carried off his intellectual legs by the sensational eschatology of Schweitzer. It was a misfortune that he seems to have been unable to derive much intellectual satisfaction from any modern system of Philosophy. He did no doubt read a good deal in this direction; but when once his confidence in tradition and in Scholasticism was destroyed, his mind wandered vaguely about in a somewhat rudderless condition. It is difficult to say what his final position was. His utterances are not always consistent. But the following passage from a letter to a French correspondant may be taken as an unusually definite statement:

" What I find in myself as the highest law and law-giver of my being, is a Divine Will or Ideal, which struggles to realise itself against a contrary and disintegrating tendency; and does so independently of my co-operation. I recognise it as the same will which moves every living creature, and indeed the whole world, towards its proper perfection and highest development. Religions can help one to name it, to imagine it, to understand it, to converse with it. I learn to call it Conscience, my better self, the Holy Spirit, the indwelling Christ. As pervading or transcending all creation, I call it the Eternal Father, source of all being; as working in myself and in the heart of men, I call it the Holy Spirit; as giving me an outward rule, model, example of idealised and divinised humanity in Christ (and in His saints), I call it the Son of

God. And these three are manifestations of one and the same thing, or Will, or Spirit which I call God." [1]

In spite of some ambiguities of language, this confession of faith (dated January 11, 1908) is a fairly definite Christian Theism. In face of such a declaration one is inclined to wonder why Tyrrell should talk so much about Divine Immanence, and distinguish himself so sharply from the believers in an' " outside God." A will which transcends as well as pervades all creation is as " outside a God " as anyone believes in who has ceased to think of Him as literally inhabiting a local Heaven. But he was not always so definite. Take, for instance, such an utterance as this on January 18, 1909:

> " Houtin and Loisy are right, the Christianity of the future will consist of mysticism and charity, and possibly the Eucharist in its primitive form as the outward bond." [2]

It is true that mysticism may be meant to include Theism, but even so the fact that the belief in God should not be explicitly mentioned is significant.

I do not myself believe that the type of mind revealed by *Christianity at the Cross-roads* can have any great future. I cannot believe that any considerable body of men will believe that Jesus uttered all the eschatological sayings attributed to Him, that they represent a simple delusion, and yet that this delusion must ever be the essence of Christianity—to be accepted literally (it would seem) by the vulgar, by the initiated as a symbol of some vague hope for a future life; that they will regard all the ethical teaching of Christ with something very like contempt as a mere *Interimsethik,* and most of the religious teaching too (except the admitted delusions), and yet continue passionately Christian; that they will share all the negative beliefs of rationalistic Protestants,

[1] Vol. II, 413 f.   [2] Vol. II, 377.

and yet continue ardent Catholics; that they will take a grimly pessimistic view of this world's present and future, and yet continue to believe in a God who cares for Humanity, and found on that belief their hope of Immortality. Contradictions like these are explainable psychologically as the momentary, half-despairing, half-trustful attitude of a sorely puzzled seeker after truth whose emotions cleave to the illusions which his Reason has abandoned; but it is inconceivable that either the Roman or any other " Catholic " Church which adopted such an attitude can have any considerable influence over mankind.

Still less capable of any but a psychological explanation is Tyrrell's attitude towards Protestanism. Perhaps the greatest value of Tyrrell's *Life* and writings at the present moment lies in his keen appreciation of the defects of Protestantism, as Protestantism is understood by German Liberal theologians. He understood the meaning of the words Church, Worship, Sacrament as hardly any continental Protestant understands them; and he may help English-speaking Liberals to avoid the mistakes of their continental masters. I am not myself without sympathy for the positive side of Tyrrell's attitude. But that a " Catholic " so broadminded in his feeling towards other religions as to keep a Buddha under his crucifix should have brought himself to write that—

> " Jesus would say Harnack was *not far from* the Kingdom of God, but that a miss was as good as a mile; that ' there was no difference between Protestants and savages; all would burn in hell alike ' " [1]

—this can only be explained by the prejudices of temperament and early association. I share the belief that the next great religious movement, if there is one, will have to run on lines considerably different from those of continental Liberal Protestantism, but

[1] Vol. II, 400.

Tyrrell's failure to appreciate Protestantism, and (I may add) that side of Christ's own teaching which Protestantism really understands, seems to me to vitiate all Tyrrell's later writing upon the present and future of Christianity. Of course many passages of quite a contrary tendency will be found in his works, and in one respect Tyrrell, we may almost say, was a Protestant all his life, whether he knew it or not. Nobody ever claimed and exercised more vigorously the right of private judgement.

It is impossible to read these volumes without feeling a profound respect for the life-work of a sincere pilgrim in search of truth, who suffered much in its pursuit. Even to those who (like the present critic) know him only through his *Life* and his writings, he will appear an extremely attractive and lovable personality. But, as there is a tendency in some quarters to make Tyrrell more of a prophet than he is, I will say candidly that I do not think a great deal of intellectual guidance is to be derived from his *Life* or writings. There are no doubt flashes of very deep insight, but hardly a consistent, thought-out attitude towards the religious problems of our day. He may for a time help not a few souls in distress—especially those who have once believed in the Roman system or in very High Anglicanism—to cling to religious hopes and practices at moments when the lamp of faith burns low, and he will assist readers of a more Protestant tendency to appreciate the stronger side of Catholicism; but it is on the side of devotion and of religious feeling rather than of strictly intellectual illumination that Tyrrell will help forward that movement towards a new Reformation for which he laboured so strenuously. The devotional writings of what Miss Petre calls this " middle Jesuit period " are among the few definitely devotional writings in which the reader will find little or nothing out of harmony with an essentially modern view of the universe.

IX

THE ATONEMENT [1]

THE greatest defect which I discover in most
modern attempts at a re-statement of the traditional
doctrine of the Atonement is that the writers begin
to ask what is the meaning of the doctrine without
inquiring into its history—or at least into the earliest
period of that history. Writers who would not for
a moment deliberately maintain the doctrine of verbal
or even plenary inspiration or the equal authority
of all parts of the New Testament practically assume
that there is a doctrine of the Atonement—one single
doctrine, always the same and of equal authority—
which is absolutely binding, and has somehow got
to be explained and defended. They are often eager
to repudiate all those explanations of the doctrine
which are most repulsive to the moral consciousness of
modern Christians, if they very often end by bringing
them back in disguised and attenuated forms. They
will reject and disparage the more liberal interpretations of the doctrine on the ground that they explain
away something which is of its essence, without asking
themselves whether what they insist on does not come
to us from exactly the same authority as the features
which they reject. They will sometimes pick and
choose very freely among the Patristic and Scholastic
representations of these matters, accepting what they
like and rejecting what they dislike; but as regards
the New Testament they practically assume that one
and the same doctrine is found in all parts of it, and
that all that is found in the New Testament doctrines
is equally binding upon us. Sometimes this procedure
is justified by a distinction between the fact of the
Atonement and the theory of it; but such writers
forget to ask how far what is called the fact does
not really imply a theory. Practically they treat all
the actual words of St. Paul as belonging to the fact
which must be taken as a datum, and theory is only

[1] A paper read to the Origen Society at Oxford, March 1917.

142

supposed to begin when we come to the further elaboration of St. Paul's thought. This system frequently ends in reading a great deal into other parts of the New Testament which is not there, and ignoring or explaining away much of what is to be found in St. Paul. Philosophers have contributed to this unjustifiable procedure as well as theologians—in some ways more so. They assume that an intelligible, reasonable, defensible meaning has somehow got to be found in the doctrine with little or no inquiry into the question from what source it has come to us, and what it really meant to those who originally formulated it. This tendency has been increased by the fact that among German Lutherans the doctrine of the Atonement has come to be treated as the central doctrine of Christianity. Minds which have long since repudiated all other traditional doctrines, even that of the Divinity of our Lord, are still in bondage to Luther, and this bondage compels them also to treat St. Paul in a way which contrasts markedly with the freedom of their attitude towards every other early Christian authority, even though St. Paul may in the end be treated after all only as a not quite unintelligent anticipator of Luther.

Surely every thorough-going inquiry into the paramount meaning of the doctrine must begin with an inquiry into its origin. We must on no account assume that a doctrine is not true because it is not contained in the teaching of our Lord or of the earliest Christian teachers. The Ritschlians are, as it seems to me, profoundly wrong and profoundly unphilosophical in rejecting the principle of development. Nor is a doctrine necessarily without meaning or significance for us because the grounds on which it was historically accepted are grounds of which we can no longer admit the validity. It is highly probable that the doctrine of human immortality would never have occurred to anyone but for the phenomena of dreams; and yet Plato, or a modern philosopher, may accept the doctrine on quite other grounds. So it may be with any other traditional doctrine of Christianity. So, I myself believe, it is with the doctrine that sins are forgiven through the death of Christ. But though a doctrine may be true which is not to be discovered in the teaching of our Lord, or even any part of the New Testament, our attitude towards it, the freedom of interpretation which we allow ourselves in regard to it, the importance of the place which we assign to it in our general view of Christianity, may be profoundly affected by the source from which it comes to us and the grounds upon which it commended itself to the first originators.

I proceed then to ask, " Is there any basis in the teaching of our Lord for the doctrine that sins are forgiven by God in consequence of the death of Christ, for that reason only, and on condition of belief that they are so forgiven? " Here—and, indeed, in the rest of this paper—I must ask you to excuse for the sake of brevity an enormous amount of unlicensed dogmatism. I can only give you conclusions, not, indeed, without a glance at the reasons for them, but without developing these reasons or replying to inevitable objections. I need hardly apologise for putting aside the Fourth Gospel in a matter in which everything depends upon our being able to assume that we have before us the *ipsissima verba* of Christ, though this is not done by many modern writers— notably the late Dr. Moberly—who could never in cold blood have defended the critical position involved in such a treatment. In the Synoptic Gospels our Lord nowhere teaches the forgiveness of sins as dependent upon the fact of His death. And He does teach a doctrine which is wholly inconsistent with that doctrine. In the parable of the Prodigal Son, in that of the Pharisee and the Publican, and in fact everywhere He teaches that sins are forgiven upon the one sole condition of sincere repentance—which includes, of course, a measure of amendment wherever the opportunity for amendment is given. It would simply not be true that the publican went down to his house justified if he could only obtain justification through an historical event which had not yet occurred or through believing in that historical event of which he would have never heard.

There are only two passages which can possibly be quoted to show that our Lord ever claimed to teach differently. The first of these is the famous assertion: " and to give His life a ransom for many." In view of the fact that these words are not found in Luke, who in the rest of the sayings agrees with Matthew-Mark, it is, to my mind, very doubtful indeed whether our Lord uttered them. If He did, they must clearly be interpreted in a way which makes them harmonious, and not in a way which makes them totally inconsistent with the rest of His teaching. That the suffering or death of the righteous helps surviving Israelites, that such sufferings are in some sense treated by God as an additional reason for extending His mercy to Israel at large, was a familiar Jewish idea. The classical expression of it is the great passage about the Suffering Servant in the Second Isaiah. It is conceivable though quite unprovable that our Lord may have applied to Himself the language of Isaiah, whether or not He understood, as the Jews in general did not understand, the Servant of Jehovah to mean, definitely and exclusively, the Messiah. But to say that for a moment the thought that perhaps the death of the Messiah might help towards the spiritual emancipation of many in Israel—not, be it observed, all Israel or all mankind—is a very different thing from the declaration that sins could only be forgiven in this way, and that His death was to be accepted by God as a punishment or a sacrifice or expiation for the sins of the whole world, which was otherwise doomed to an eternity of woe. We can only understand the saying in this latter sense by making this solitary and doubtful utterance totally inconsistent with the whole body of the Master's well-authenticated teaching. Of the doctrine that forgiveness was to be dependent upon belief in this atoning efficacy of Christ's death there is, it is needless to say, no trace, even in the saying about the ransom.

There is only one other word attributed to our Lord which calls for a moment's notice. The account of the Last Supper contains many inconsistencies between the four narratives, many differences of text, many difficulties of interpretation; but no view of these matters will establish anything as regards our particular problem beyond the fact that Jesus regarded His death as a death of self-sacrifice for His followers, if we put aside the words " for the remission of sins " which occur only in the First Gospel, and belong to the large category of " ecclesiastical additions " which are found in the present text of that Gospel.

How and when did the idea arise that sins could be forgiven only through the death of Christ? Many people, even now—outside the circle of professional theologians—will be disposed to suggest: " It is the invention of St. Paul." Such a theory is rendered absolutely impossible by a single sentence in St. Paul's own writings. " Christ died for our sins according to the Scriptures." This, St. Paul declares, was part of what he received, part of the tradition of the Church into which he was baptised, already part of the established Creed of that Church. The words, as it seems to me, contain the clue to the whole matter. Both halves of the sentence are equally significant: it was for our sins that Christ died, and it was in accordance with the Scriptures that He died for sins. Where do the Scriptures say that the Messiah was to die and die for sins? In the light of the earliest Christian literature, no one can have any hesitation in pointing primarily to the great passage about the Suffering Servant in *Isaiah* 53. There, in a book which the early Christians regarded as plenarily inspired in the fullest and most literal sense, we find it stated that the chastisement of our peace was upon him, that by his stripes we should be healed, that his soul should be made an offering for sin. The ignominious death of a Son of God was the great stumbling-block of early Christianity. We know how for the moment it undermined the belief of the Apostles themselves; it was the greatest obstacle to the acceptance of the Gospel by Greek as well as Jew. The great puzzle of the early Christian Apologist was to account for it. What a solution to all his difficulties when he discovered from the 53rd of *Isaiah* that it had been prophesied that this must be so, and that it was in this way that sin was to be forgiven. The solution was completely in harmony with the preconceived ideas both of Jew and of Gentile, though especially of the Gentile whom the usage of sacrifice and in particular the Mysteries had familiarised with the idea that the death of a hero-god might possess an atoning efficacy. It was hardly possible that any early Christian could read that great chapter without applying it in his own mind to his crucified Lord, and when once the application was made, it was simply inevitable, in the then state of religious thought, that it should take possession of the Church and become part of its traditional inheritance.

This view of the matter is strongly supported by the references to the death of Christ in the earliest Christian literature. No one can read that literature carefully without noticing two things: (1) that the notion of a vicarious punishment or expiation or any sort of objective atonement is entirely absent, except in actual quotations from *Isaiah* 53 or other Old Testament Scriptures or in short, traditional formulae based upon the words of the Old Testament and amounting to virtual quotations. We constantly read that Christ died for us, that we are forgiven or cleansed through His blood, or the like. But when any explanation of such phrases is attempted, the explanation is always something ethical, intelligible, and quite unlike the later doctrines which were based upon the prophetic language. (2) Much more frequently than not salvation is attributed, not specifically to the death of Christ, but to His coming, His preaching, His example, His revelation of the Father, His Resurrection; but where the necessity and the efficacy of Christ's death are specially dwelt upon, it is accounted for in one of the following ways:

(*a*) The death of Christ was necessary simply that prophecy should be fulfilled.

(*b*) It was the necessary pre-condition of the Resurrection. Very often when an early Christian speaks of being saved by Christ's death, he really means (I am persuaded) being saved by His Resurrection. The proposition that the Resurrection and not the death of Christ was the centre of the earliest Gospel is strongly supported by the contents of the early speeches in Acts. The later you put the composition of those speeches, the more significant becomes the fact.

(*c*) It was necessary to prove the reality of Christ's human body and so refute Docetism.

(*d*) It was a revelation of the love of God, moving the heart of men to gratitude, imitation, and answering love—the crowning and typical event in a whole life of love—based upon certain passages of Scripture.

(*e*) Occasionally there are traces of the idea—based upon certain passages of Scripture—that Christ's death, in some unexplained way, weakened and defeated the evil spirits, though the notion is so vague that at present it hardly amounts to a distinct theory. Moreover, this triumph over the powers of evil is rarely attributed to the death exclusively, but rather to Christ's life-long resistance to temptation, and to the Resurrection.

In the earliest writers up to and including Justin, there is no explanation of the death of Christ going beyond the bare stock formulae which does not fall under one of these heads—with one single exception, and that is St. Paul.

By the great mass of early Christians the doctrine that sins were to be forgiven through the death of Christ was accepted simply on authority. It was not based by them on anything which Christ had taught. It was not, as is often suggested, due in the first instance to Christian experience. When once it was accepted, there was abundance of experience which seemed to confirm it. The saving effects of Christ's work as a whole—of His teaching, of the revelation of God in Him, of the hopes based upon His Resurrection—these, indeed, were matters of direct experience; but that the moral revolution in his whole being of which the early Christian was conscious was due primarily to Christ's death—this could not well be the result of experience. This was a *theory* which, from the nature of the case, could not be due to experience; it was a theory which attempted to explain and account for the experience. For most simple-minded Christians the belief rested upon authority pure and simple: it had been revealed by God to Isaiah, and that was a sufficient reason for believing it. No Christian who was not prepared to side with the Marcionites and the Gnostics against the Old Testament could possibly deny it. But everyone was free to explain it as he pleased. The simple Christian needed no theory to explain it. That the forgiveness of sins should be effected by a sacrifice was an idea completely in harmony with ancient ways of thinking. More thoughtful Christians did feel the need of explanation. They constructed theories about it, if they are so simple as hardly to be called theories. The early theories are, if we except the defeat of the evil spirits, thoroughly ethical and intelligible. They fully account for and justify the saving influ-

149

ence which is attributed to Christ and His work as a whole; though no doubt they seem hardly to justify the sacrificial or substitutionary Old Testament language which they are put forward to explain. They hardly account for the extreme prominence which the traditional phrases attach to the death of Christ— as distinct from His Incarnation in general, His life, His teaching, His Resurrection. Or at least there is only one of the explanations which really does so; and that is the insistence upon the gratitude which is called forth by the death of the innocent Son— not, indeed, by the death alone, but by the death treated as the typical and crowning act of a whole life of love and self-sacrifice.

What has been said as to the treatment of the Atonement in the earliest extra-canonical writers is equally true, I think, of the canonical writers, with the single exception of St. Paul. Everywhere we meet with the traditional phrases about the death of Christ, and with ethical and rational explanations. The first epistle attributed to St. Peter is a good illustration—Christ suffered for sins once; but the death of Christ is immediately treated as an example to His followers, who were also called upon to suffer for righteousness' sake. The Johannine writings treat the death of Christ mainly as a revelation of the love of God: "Greater love hath no man than this, that a man should lay down his life for his friends." There is nothing substitutionary or expiatory about the writer's ideas beyond the bare use of the traditional word "propitiation" and the other traditional phrases.

But what of St. Paul? There, indeed, we do find an attempt to construct a very elaborate theory of the Atonement. In teaching that Christ died for our sins, St. Paul was simply handing on the common faith of the Church; his explanation as to why Christ had to suffer, and as to how the benefits of His death are to be appropriated, is his own. And I am

afraid it is necessary to admit that St. Paul does
teach the doctrine of substitution. Sacrificial language is, indeed, rarely used, and never without some
consciousness of metaphor. St. Paul's ideas are for
the most part not sacrificial, but juridical. And
it is impossible to get rid of the fact—I long tried
to think to the contrary, but I have been forced to
admit it—that St. Paul does deliberately teach that
sin necessarily brings death (whether through some
intrinsic necessity of things or simply on account of
God's threat to our first parents), and that the innocent Christ bore the penalty instead of the guilty
and that therefore in some constructive or legal sense
all humanity, or all believers, have borne it too. The
word " punishment " is not actually used; but something which cannot well be otherwise described is
implied in such passages as " God sending His own
Son, in the likeness of sinful flesh and as an offering
for sin, condemned sin in the flesh " (Rom. viii. 3),
and " he was made a curse for us." To a certain
point, indeed, what has been said of the other writers
may be said of St. Paul too: he simply accepts the
fact that Christ died for sins, on authority. And he
never really does explain fully why sins could not be
forgiven except by the death of Christ. But, unlike
the other writers, he does—not, indeed, primarily for
the purpose of proving the efficacy of Christ's death,
but for the purpose of establishing his great doctrine of
Gentile liberty—involve himself in rabbinical arguments which really imply that the penalty due to sin
was transferred to Christ. The value that he attaches
to the fact is mainly the exhibition of the love of
God which it involves; but the necessity for the penal
infliction, which for him was proved by the plenarily
inspired Old Testament, is certainly in the background
of all his thought on the subject. We do not in
other matters consider ourselves bound by every
opinion of St. Paul. We do not accept his beliefs
about the historical fact of the Fall, about the in-

spiration of the Old Testament, and about the Divine authority of the Law. We do not now consider ourselves bound to accept his rabbinical interpretations of Scripture, or the rabbinic logic with which he applies them—his explanation that the rock in the wilderness is Christ or that Hagar is Mount Sinai in Arabia or the argument which he bases upon the distinction between seed and seeds. It is time surely that we should candidly admit that there is an element in St. Paul's teaching about the death of Christ and its justifying effects which we cannot accept. It is a small element in the actual teaching of St. Paul, but unfortunately it is just the side of his teaching to which later theological systems have given an extreme and most disastrous prominence. Most of what St. Paul teaches about the justifying effects in Christ's work is quite intelligible without the idea of an objective expiation.

The small influence which was at first exercised by the special and characteristic teaching of St. Paul is one of the strangest facts in ecclesiastical history. The teaching of the earliest Fathers about the death of Christ and about justification is, as I have already shown, very little influence by St. Paul's ideas. And this continued to be the case to a large extent long after there could be any question about the authority of St. Paul's writings. Hardly before St. Augustine do we find a theology which is based mainly upon St. Paul. No doubt in some quite early writers—at least from the time of Justin—we do find St. Paul's statements formally accepted just like the Old Testament statements on which they rested; but, like those statements, they were still largely explained in an ethical and rational manner. The difficult things are ignored or explained away. But from the time of Irenaeus begin the theories which attempt to give a more literal meaning and a more elaborate explanation to St. Paul's statements about the death of Christ. The old ethical ways of thinking and speaking are not, indeed, abandoned, but others are added to them. I will not attempt to enumerate here all the theories about the death of Christ which are discoverable in the works of Irenaeus; but I will just notice the two most prominent lines of thought. In the first place, we have the theory of the transaction with the Devil. The passage in the Gospels about the ransom suggested the question to whom the ransom was paid. And the answer which best fitted in with early Christian ideas was that the ransom must have been paid to the Devil. By the sin of man mankind had become the slave of Satan. It would have been unjust for God to have released men from bondage to him. So God contrived a plan by which justice to the Devil should be made compatible with mercy to fallen man. By bringing about the death of Christ the Devil claimed more than his due: Christ was innocent; the Devil had no claim to that life. Hence it became just for God by way of set-off to take back fallen man from the dominion of Satan and to remit the penalty which he had incurred by sin. Two elements in the system were emphasised and elaborated by later writers (Tertullian and others) more so than they are in Irenaeus—first, the justice of men's captivity to the Devil, which Irenaeus sometimes denies; and, secondly, the element of deception involved in the arrangement adopted by God. The Devil was led to believing that by bringing about the death of Christ he would be completing his empire over humanity, whereas this really became the means of his defeat. This notion of a trick on the part of God became in popular thought the prominent element in the matter, and expressed itself in the childish conceit—which we find in such writers as Rufinus, Gregory of Nyssa, and Gregory the Great—that the humanity of Christ was the bait which the Devil, like a greedy fish, eagerly swallowed and so became impaled upon the hook of His Divinity.

The other theory which starts with Irenaeus is the

theory of Recapitulation. By the union between God and Man in Christ humanity was restored to the perfection for which God had originally intended His creature man, but which had been lost by the Fall. By the influence of this union man was brought back into that union with and likeness to God which Irenaeus does not hesitate to describe as an actual deification. God becomes man that men might become gods. This theory carries with it—if it is, indeed, the essence of his meaning—the restoration of his immortality forfeited by sin. So far the theory is a theory rather of the Incarnation than of the Atonement, in that narrower sense in which the forgiveness of sins is supposed to flow especially from the death of Christ. And in Irenaeus as in all his Greek successors this is the main thought: what they really believed in was salvation by the Incarnation, including the Resurrection and glorification of Christ. But still the traditional language about the death of Christ had to be justified, and it was a subordinate feature of the theory —faintly suggested by Irenaeus and more strongly emphasised by later writers—that not only did the effects of Christ's life of perfect holiness and obedience extend to humanity at large, but also the effects of His death. In Christ humanity paid the penalty due to sin, and so each individual human being, united to Christ by faith and baptism, might be deemed really to have paid it, and so to have satisfied the claims of Divine justice.

Nearly all the later theories about the Atonement may be traced back to these two sources. I must not attempt even to set forth that later history in detail; but I should like to say a word about each of them.

(1) I will begin with the last—with what is characteristically the Greek theory of Redemption, though it is not actually confined to Eastern theology. In Irenaeus and his best successors—in such men as Athanasius or the far more philosophical Gregory of Nyssa—there is a perpetual oscillation between the

two different interpretations of the vague language
which they employ about the consequences of the
bringing together of the Godhead and the Manhood
in Christ. Sometimes the effects seem to spring from
the actual moral influence of Christ—of His teaching,
His example, His revelation of the character of God,
of the self-sacrificing love inspired by Christ's death,
of the hopes inspired by the Resurrection. In this
view of the matter there is contained, as I venture to
think, the whole truth both about the Incarnation in
general and about the special effects of Christ's death.
As a matter of simple experience these effects are
amply sufficient to justify the traditional language
of the Church about the saving effects of Christ's
work and even about the saving effects of His death
when these last are not understood—as in the Greek
Fathers they never were understood—in such sense
as to exclude the rest of Christ's work from any share
in the Redemption which He effected. And in the
best of the Greeks this interpretation is uppermost.
It is so even in Irenaeus. On the other hand, there
are in his writings traces of a view which becomes
much more prominent in his successors. The Incarnation and, in some paramount and yet generally
unexplained way, the death of Christ are thought
of as actually setting up by a direct metaphysical
or almost physical influence a process in the bodies
and souls of men which converts the corruptible flesh
into an incorruptible body. Even in this life the body
and soul of the believer may now be regarded as in
some sense incorruptible, and the process eventually
culminates in the completely incorruptible state of
the resurrection body, the process being effected mainly
through the Sacraments. The contact in Christ of
the universal " Humanity " with the universal " Divinity " transforms the human substance into the likeness of the Divine; this is what is now primarily
meant by Deification. In Origen the ethical interpretation of Deification is, I think it may fairly be

said, the only one, though of course he holds that the soul that becomes like God in holiness is also eternal. In the best of his successors the metaphysical or quasi-physical interpretation is continually struggling with the ethical. As time goes on, it gradually gains upon it, and at last, in the typical Greek theologian John of Damascus, it becomes practically the only interpretation. And by this time the metaphysic has degenerated into something which must be regarded as not far removed from pure thaumaturgy.

The line of thought by which this last combination is reached is, of course, a monstrous abuse of the Platonic doctrine of Universals. It is assumed that whatever influence is exercised on the one Man Jesus Christ by the union of the two universals, extends also to all other individuals of the class who have complied with the proper requirements—for the most part purely sacramental, though certain conditions of belief and a certain minimum of morality are necessary to enable the Sacraments to work. As a part of this theory we get a very definite explanation of the necessary effects of Christ's death. It is explained that the whole humanity which sinned has now paid the penalty ordained by God, and consequently each individual who satisfies the conditions has really paid it too, and is entitled to the verdict of acquittal, as regards the entail of original sin, though final salvation has to be won largely by his own efforts.

This monstrous theory, attenuated and disguised in various forms, is really at the bottom of most of the theories about the death of Christ which are current among us even at the present day, though they are now for the most part so much watered down that the logical fallacy which they involve becomes less obvious. In order that you may see how completely the theory turns upon a sheer logical fallacy, I will quote from John of Damascus the passage in which it is most systematically expounded.

"Essence ($ov\sigma\iota a$) is predicated of the individual: therefore in each individual of the species the essence is perfect (or complete). Therefore neither do the individuals differ from one another in essence, but only in respect of the accidents which are their characteristic properties. For they define the individual as 'essence together with accidents.' So that the individual has what is common together with that which individualises it, besides existing substantially in itself. But the essence does not exist substantially in itself, but is only seen in the individuals. When, then, one of the individuals suffers, all the essence, in respect of which the individual has suffered, so far as it is capable of suffering, is said to have suffered in one of its individuals; without, however, its being necessary that all the individuals of the same species should suffer with the individual that actually suffers."[1]

It is surely needless to point out the fallacy which underlies this theory. It is not true that to suffer crucifixion belongs to the essence of the class "man." It is essentially an accident. It is as absurd to argue that all men or all Christians have suffered the penalty of crucifixion because Jesus Christ did so, as it would be to say that all men were born in Bethlehem because Christ was born in Bethlehem, or that all are Jews because Christ was a Jew. As to the modern language about Christ being actually "the universal of humanity," the logical absurdity involved in this assertion is something of which even John of Damascus would have been ashamed. A universal cannot be a particular member of the class indicated by the class-name. If such a statement means merely that Christ represents in an unique or supreme degree the ideal of humanity, it would be better to say so, and to give up this

[1] *Expositio Fidei Orthodoxae*, iii, 6. [The Greek text is given in Rashdall's *Idea of Atonement in Christian Theology*, p. 318n. —Edd.]

attempt to go beyond the Dark Ages in the revival of a bastard Platonism.

(2) I will now turn to the other element in the Patristic theory about the death of Christ—the theory of the ransom paid to the Devil, which likewise originated with Irenaeus. That theory is found in almost all writers after Irenaeus and Tertullian—though not, I think, in Origen. Origen's language approaches this theory, but the similarity is only apparent; he describes in language which is partly metaphysical the Devil's momentary victory and then Christ's lasting triumph over the Devil without any attempt to show that such a death was demanded by justice to the Devil. But it is found in most of the great Greek Fathers, and more or less implied by the language even when it is not set forth in express terms. Gregory of Nazianzus is the only one who utters a word of definite protest. But in the Greeks the theory is not prominent. The other view is the prominent one: their theology centres in the Incarnation, not in the Atonement. The transaction with the Devil was just a tradition which had to be accepted, but was of little interest to metaphysical minds. It is in the Western Fathers that the theory occupies the most prominent position.

For some nine hundred years this theory was the orthodox theory on the subject—in the West at least the very central point of orthodoxy. Those who consider themselves bound by a *consensus patrum* ought to hold this doctrine. No doctrine which excludes this view has the same claim to be considered the orthodox theory. And yet never in the whole history of Christian thought has a doctrine been so decidedly destroyed by criticism and more universally abandoned. This revolution in Christian thought was due to the influence of two great thinkers—Anselm and Abelard. Anselm formally denied that Christ's death was a penalty paid to the Devil, or that the Devil had become the lawful Sovereign of man instead of

God; the theory shocked him by its obvious profanity. Anselm was a great personage—in other respects unimpeachably orthodox; consequently he escaped any formal censure. But when the same denial was made by that much bolder thinker—and I must add less edifying character—Abelard, it provoked a violent storm of opposition, the protagonist of which was the great St. Bernard, who united in his own person all that was best and all that was most odious in the character of the medieval saint. Acting under his influence, the transaction with the Devil was definitely affirmed by the Council of Sens in 1141, and by St. Bernard's creature, Pope Innocent III. They do not seem to have been aware that they were condemning Anselm as much as Abelard.

But no doubt the Council had this much justification, that the theory which Anselm set up in place of the ransom-theory, though the grotesqueness and profanity of the old view were avoided, was at bottom just as immoral and irrational as the one which he discarded. Anselm merely substituted an impersonal Justice for a personal Devil. Abelard, on the other hand, provided the medieval world with a theory to which no objection can be taken on moral grounds. It is the view of Christ's death which can really claim the largest consensus not only of Fathers but of Christians from the earliest days to the latest—the view which simply treats the death of Christ as a peculiarly characteristic and conspicuous exhibition of that self-sacrificing love which was the inspiring motive of all Christ's work for man and which makes it the great revelation of God. moving the world to answering love and gratitude. I cannot do better than quote to you Abelard's words:

" I think that the purpose and cause of the Incarnation was that He might illuminate the world by His wisdom and excite it to the love of Himself." [1]

[1]. *Opera*, ed. Cousin, ii, 767. [The Latin of this and the following passages will be found in Rashdall's *Idea of Atonement*, pp. 362 ff.—EDD.]

Here is a fuller explanation:

"Every man is also made juster, that is to say, becomes more loving to God after the passion of Christ than he was before, because a benefit actually received kindles the soul into love more than one merely hoped for. Our redemption, therefore, is that supreme love of Christ shown to us by His passion which not only frees us from slavery to sin, but acquires for us the true liberty of the sons of God, so that we fulfil all things from love of Him rather than from fear." [1]

Here is another fine passage:

"To us it appears that we are none the less justified in the blood of Christ, and reconciled to God by this singular grace exhibited to us, that His Son took our nature, and in it took upon Himself to instruct us alike by word and example even unto death (and so) bound us to Himself by love, that kindled by so great a benefit of divine grace, charity should not be afraid to endure anything for His sake; which benefit indeed we do not doubt, kindled the ancient fathers also, who expected this by faith, into supreme love of God no less than the men of (this) time." [2]

Abelard is a reputed heretic, but in this and in many other ways his theory rapidly won its way to general, though not universal, acceptance. Side by side with other theories—often wholly inconsistent with it—it is, indeed, held by all Christians. Without such inconsistent additions it was adopted by Abelard's great disciple, Peter the Lombard, whose *Book of the Sentences* was throughout the Middle Ages the authorised text-book of theology, the one theological book which was set side by side with the Bible as the subject of lectures. It was taught by the first great Oxford theologian, Robert Pullen, who

[1] *Opera,* ed. Cousin, ii, 207.
[2] *Opera,* ed. Cousin, ii, 767.

became a Cardinal and Chancellor of the Holy Roman Church. And there can be little doubt that, if he had preserved to us the theological lectures of the Abelardian Pope Celestine II we should find him teaching the same simple and wholly ethical doctrine.

I have left myself no time either for the discussion of the theories which I have rejected or for defending the view of the Atonement which it is the object of this paper to commend to you. I shall leave the noble words of Abelard and the Master of the Sentences to commend themselves to you on their own merits. If anyone is anxious as to the orthodoxy of the doctrine, I do not know why anybody should wish to be more orthodox than Peter the Lombard. I will merely sum up very briefly the positions which I have tried to establish.

(1) It may be treated as certain (whether or not we treat the ransom-passage as genuine) that our Lord Himself never taught the doctrine that His death was an atonement for sin. He consistently taught that God forgives sin on the one condition of true penitence—that is to say, the turning of the will to God. Any doctrine of the Atonement which is to be really Christian must be consistent with this fundamental truth.

(2) The traditional language about the saving effects of Christ's death was based upon the authority of Old Testament prophecy, and cannot be considered eternally binding on Christians who do not accept the Jewish view as to the plenary inspiration of the Old Testament or the early Christian interpretation of it, except in so far as a rational and ethical meaning —a meaning consistent with our Lord's own teaching —can be found for it.

(3) Such a meaning was found for it by the early Christian writers, who explain it by the regenerating influence exercised by Christ's work as a whole. They account for the special prominence of His death by the fact that in a supreme way it exhibits the love of

God, and excites the repentance and desire of imitation which that love awakens. " Greater love hath no man than this."

(4) St. Paul is the only New Testament writer who can be said to teach the doctrine that Christ bore the punishment of sin instead of us. We are not bound by this teaching, which was not really accepted by many of the best Christian Fathers.

(5) Most of the teaching of the Greek Fathers about the saving effects of Christ's death as a part of it is wholly acceptable to the modern mind, so long as it is understood of the influence which Christ's work exercised in making men really better—the only way in which the sins of the world can really be taken away.

(6) We cannot, however, accept the theory that either the Incarnation or the death of Christ really transforms a corruptible into an incorruptible body, or that every human being can be said to have paid the penalty of sin because Christ paid it.

(7) We cannot accept the theory that the death of Christ was required by justice to the Devil, or the Anselmian modification which regarded it as due to the necessity that abstract justice demanded such a sacrifice.

(8) Abelard and his followers really return to the more primitive and ethical teaching of the earliest Fathers and of the best Greek teachers such as Origen, and present us with a view of the Atonement which is entirely compatible with the requirements of Reason and Conscience and with the teaching of our Lord Himself. Christ taught that the Father is always ready to accept the sinner on the one condition of repentance and amendment. The Abelardian teaching is wholly in accordance with this teaching inasmuch as it represents Christ's life and death, the Revelation of God, as the strongest influence which there is in the world for bringing about that repentance and amendment upon which, as He Himself taught, acceptance with God really depends.

X

THE SCHOLASTIC THEOLOGY [1]

I SUSPECT there are a good many people who do not associate many definite ideas with that mysterious group of writers generally known as the Schoolmen beyond remembering that (according to our XXXIX Articles) they " vainly talk," i.e. about one particular subject—the efficacy of good works. Many others whose knowledge goes a good deal further than this may still be a little vague and confused on the subject. It may therefore be well to begin at the beginning and attempt to explain exactly what is meant by the term " Scholastic Theology," even at the risk of saying nothing that is not already familiar to most educated persons, beyond a few expressions of personal opinion with which they may possibly not agree.

In the first place, it may be well to clear up the distinction between the Scholastic Theology and the Scholastic Philosophy. The philosophy presupposed by most of the Fathers is Platonism or more correctly neo-Platonism, i.e. the philosophy of Plotinus and his followers. That was notoriously the case with St. Augustine. And the theology of the West was mainly built up upon that of St. Augustine. This philosophy was largely that of the Eastern Fathers also. In the Patristic period the influence of Aristotle is more discernible in the less orthodox theologians than in those orthodox writers who have come to be considered Fathers of the Church. And all through the Dark Ages, Western Theology was based mainly upon the teaching of the Fathers. At the same time there was one element in the teaching of Aristotle which formed a large element in the ordinary secular education of the West, so far as any education at all survived: and that was his Logic. During this period— extending (say) from the Sixth to the middle of the Twelfth Century—the whole of the Aristotelian writings were lost except a fragment of his Logic, i.e. the

[1] This paper was apparently read to a Clerical Society.

De Interpretatione and the *Categories* (or during a portion of that period only an abridgment of the *Categories*). The rest of the *Organon* was known only indirectly through the commentaries of Boethius, and quotations or references to his opinions in Macrobius and other authors. Still, in that way, the Aristotelian Logic—especially Aristotle's doctrine of the Syllogism—formed an important element in Dark-Age education. All through that period the question of the reality of Universals was a good deal discussed; and that question necessarily involved metaphysical issues which at times led up into theological controversy. But during the really dark period of European history there was not much connection between the Philosophy, which formed the basis of such secular education as there was, and the Theology of the time. Theology was positive or traditional—based upon authority, and especially (in the West) upon the Theology of St. Augustine with its Platonic pre-suppositions. There *was* a Scholastic Philosophy, i.e. a Philosophy taught in the Schools—mainly at this time confined to Logic—but there can hardly be said to have been a Scholastic Theology at all.

The Twelfth Century witnessed an extraordinary outburst of intellectual activity throughout Europe. The Monastic and Cathedral Schools—especially the Cathedral Schools—developed new life and vigour. And the change which this revolution brought with it involved two elements. In the first place, there was an enormous improvement and great increase in vitality in the teaching of Philosophy. At first the Philosophy was still concerned chiefly with Logic, but now the whole of the *Organon*—in a Latin translation of course—was recovered and became the subject of academic lectures. Men began to think for themselves and to discuss real questions instead of merely repeating traditional formulae. In the second place, the weapons of Logic—so long the main subject of secular education—began to be applied to Theology.

The new teachers of Philosophy began to insist on giving a reason for the faith that was in them. The attempt was made to base the main doctrines of what a later age called Natural Religion upon a rational foundation; and even to the distinctively Christian doctrines, the ultimate foundation of which was admitted to be the Bible and the traditional teaching of the Church, the weapons of Logic were applied.

Doctors trained in the Scholastic Logic began to make appeals to Reason in the exposition, the definition, and the defence of the faith. Difficulties, instead of being denied or glossed over, were developed and grappled with. Contradictions in the received authorities were keenly noticed, and an attempt was made to defend one Patristic view rather than another or to reconcile the discrepancies by ingenious distinctions. In this way the Scholastic Theology was born. The first great writer who is sometimes reckoned among the Scholastic Theologians is the famous Italian or rather Lombard Anselm, who attained enormous fame as Prior and theological teacher in the Monastery of Bec and who afterwards became Archbishop of Canterbury. In his two treatises, the *Monologion* and the *Proslogion,* he gave philosophical reasons for the belief in God; in the *Cur Deus Homo?* he developed a new Philosophy of the Atonement. Profoundly deferential as he was to the authority of Scripture, he completely threw over the theory of the Atonement which for nearly a thousand years had passed for orthodox—the theory that the death of Christ was a ransom paid to the Devil—and defended a theory which was really new: the theory of Satisfaction. In this theory at least some attempt was made to reconcile the doctrine with the requirements of Reason and Morality. But the most important innovation of Anselm was not so much any particular doctrine as the rational method by which those doctrines were defended. In the *Cur Deus Homo?* the argument is

165

conducted by means of a dialogue, which gives opportunity for the statement of objections even to the most fundamental of received opinions; and the objections are answered by an appeal to Reason, not to authority. Afterwards the form of dialogue was generally abandoned, but the leading characteristic of Anselm's teaching was retained. Objections are fully stated, urged with all the force that the writer can command, and then are met by counter-reasons. But after all, Anselm himself may be treated rather as an anticipator of the Scholastic Theology: its true founder was Abelard.

Anselm was a great philosophical thinker, but his saintly character and his deference to authority on fundamental points saved him from any charge of unorthodoxy: yet after all it was perhaps fortunate for him that he lived before the days of St. Bernard —the great adversary of the new Scholastic methods and the conclusions to which they naturally led. Abelard was a much bolder spirit than Anselm. In his *Sic et Non* the Scholastic method and the Scholastic spirit are fully developed. His attempt to construct a rational doctrine of the Holy Trinity led to his condemnation for Arianism at one Council and for Sabellianism at another—a pretty conclusive refutation of either charge. But not all the efforts of his malicious persecutor St. Bernard could succeed in putting out the conflagration which the teaching of Abelard had kindled. Abelard died a quasi-prisoner in the Monastery of Cluny—the great rival of Clairvaux—the Order which Bernard hated almost as much as he hated heresy, and whose Abbot, Peter the Venerable, did what he could to defend Abelard from the fury of the saint. Abelard was condemned; but his method and much of his actual doctrine became the basis of theological education in the now rising Universities, and especially in the great University of Paris, which grew into an organised institution through the presence of the thousands of students

and perhaps hundreds of teachers whom the fame of
Abelard had attracted to the Schools of Notre Dame.
Never was there a clearer case of the heresy of one age
becoming the orthodoxy of the next. Abelard was
condemned; but his pupil Peter the Lombard wrote
the book known as the *Sentences* which became the
recognised text-book in the theological Schools of the
Middle Ages—the only book which was placed side by
side with the Bible as the subject of academic lectures
and commentaries—and he died Bishop of Paris.
The *Sentences* may be described as an imitation, as a
more cautious version of the Abelardian treatises,
which had caused so much offence, and an extension
of the Abelardian method to the whole range of Theology. The pupil's method and to a large extent his conclusions were the same, and would have been equally
offensive to the persecutors of the master. Both of
them attempt to rationalise the doctrine of the Trinity.
With a few extremely technical differences the teaching of Abelard on the Trinity is to-day the established
doctrine of the Roman Catholic Church. Were St.
Bernard alive now, he would have been as much
shocked by the teaching which is given and the dispu-
tations which go on in every Roman Catholic seminary
as he was by the teaching of Abelard.

What I have said of the indebtedness of Peter the
Lombard to Abelard will equally apply to St. Thomas
Aquinas, the author of the great text-book the *Summa
Theologica,* which has now practically supplanted the
Lombard's *Sentences* in the teaching of the modern
Roman Catholic Church. But another great intel-
lectual change had to come over Europe before the
writing of the *Summa* could become possible. Abe-
lard and the Master of the Sentences knew nothing of
Aristotle beyond his Logic, and there is nothing in
the rules of the Syllogism which need alarm the most
susceptible orthodoxy. The controversies in which
Abelard and the Lombard engaged were controversies
within the Christian Church; there was no party or

school in Christendom which disputed the fundamentals of the Christian faith. The situation was very different when towards the end of the Twelfth Century the other works of Aristotle—his *Metaphysics,* his *Ethics,* and his books on Physics and Natural Philosophy—began to ʹfind their way into Europe. It is needless to say that on certain fundamental points the Philosophy of Aristotle was flatly at variance with the traditional teaching of the Church —much more so than the Platonic or neo-Platonic teaching which had hitherto been the chief influence in moulding its Theology. And the danger was increased by the fact that many of the works of Aristotle reached Europe at first through Oriental channels. It was the Nestorian monks or missionaries who had been driven by persecution beyond the limits of the Roman Empire to the confines of Persia who communicated the knowledge of Aristotle to the exiled Abassyd Caliphs of Baghdad. When these Abassyd Caliphs came to their own again, they took the Nestorian monks with them, and the works of Aristotle were translated into Arabic. In the Tenth Century, Baghdad became the centre of the highest culture that the world then knew. When the Moslems invaded Spain, Aristotle went with them and here a great Mohammedan Philosophy and Theology were developed. At Toledo in the Twelfth Century Aristotle—and other works of Greek Science and Philosophy—were translated into Latin. And from Spain the new Aristotle penetrated to Paris and Northern Europe. The result of this importation was an outburst of speculation of a much less orthodox and more anti-Christian character than any that hitherto had been known in medieval Christendom. And Aristotle did not travel north alone; he came accompanied by commentaries and independent works of Aristotelianising Arabic philosophers—Avicenna, Averroes, and others, including the mysterious book the *Liber de Causis,* which was mistakenly attributed to Aristotle

168

himself. Now, the Averroistic interpretation of Aristotle laid stress upon precisely those elements in the Aristotelian Philosophy which were most difficult to reconcile with the Christian faith—the eternity of the world, the unity of what was called the active intellect in God and in man, the consequent denial of personal immortality in man, and a tendency to obscure the idea of Personality in God. Sometimes the unorthodoxy disguised itself beneath a veil of Christian mysticism. Almaric of Bena maintained the apparently harmless doctrine that every believer should regard himself as a member of Christ, but it appears that that doctrine was really a cover for a more or less Pantheistic view of the relation between God and man. Among his followers this tendency was more avowed and their speculations involved a denial of transubstantiation. The first thought of alarmed orthodoxy is always repression. Almaric was either burnt or died an enforced retractation. And there were other burnings of books and of men. The condemnation did not stop short with the Commentators: it fell upon the great Master himself. In the year 1210 at a Synod held at Paris, in which Doctors of the University took part, the book of Aristotle upon Natural Philosophy and the Commentaries thereon were forbidden to be taught for a period of three years; in 1215 the *Metaphysics* fell under the same condemnation as the physical treatises. And the prohibition was repeated in 1231 by Pope Gregory IX, but with the significant reservation " until they have been examined and purged from all heresy." The theologians seem quickly to have satisfied themselves of the innocuous character of the new works: perhaps they had learned to distinguish between the genuine Aristotle and the interpretation which was put upon him by the Arabs. But certainly the purgation from all heresy never took place. It was thought better to explain—perhaps to explain away or honestly to refute—what was heretical in Aristotle than to bowdlerise him. By the middle of the century nearly the whole range of the Aristotelian writings had become the authorised text-books and by far the most important of those books used, taught, and examined in by the Master of the Arts Faculty in the rising University of Paris. And the place of the Arab-Latin translation was taken by better translations from the original Greek. Moreover, a theology was built up which re-stated the doctrine of the Church upon the basis of the new Aristotelian philosophy, so far as that could be done with doctrines already deeply tinged with Platonism. From this time onwards the Philosophy of Aristotle became the authorised Philosophy of the Church and the basis of its Theology. To prove a point of Theology it was considered enough to quote Aristotle. " The philosopher says " was the end of all controversy except upon a few points upon which it was admitted that Aristotle was corrected or at least supplemented by the Jewish or Christian Scriptures or the authority of the Church. Thus within a period of about twenty years Aristotle passed from the position of the great bugbear of all Christian thinkers into the chief pillar of the Church's philosophy and even of its Theology.

To whom was this extraordinarily rapid revolution due? Mainly to the work of the great Dominican Doctors, Albert the Great and his still more famous successor, Thomas of Aquino. The Dominican Order had been founded for the suppression of heresy—particularly of the great Albigensian heresy in the South of France with which the Almaricianism of Paris was probably not unconnected. And for purposes of suppression they were quite prepared to use force. The Inquisition was their invention, and it is probable that the Reformation—perhaps a Reformation of a much more revolutionary type—and the Renaissance would have come in the Fifteenth Century but for the activities of the Inquisition—the most cunningly devised and splendidly successful instrument for the suppression of human thought and the degradation of human character which has ever been invented. But the Dominicans, though they believed in force, believed in Reason as well. They came to the conclusion that it was well to refute heretics as well as to burn them, and better to make use of the new Philosophy even than to refute it. The world of thought had accepted Aristotle; the Church provided it with a theology based upon Aristotle. The *Summa Theologica* of St. Thomas Aquinas is the most splendid attempt which has ever been made to build up a Christian Philosophy of the Universe, to reconcile Christianity with the highest Philosophy known at the time of its production, and to defend it with the weapons of Reason.

What is the value of St. Thomas and the other Scholastic Theologians to us at the present time? I need hardly insist upon the reasons which make it impossible for us simply to adopt the *Summa*. The *Summa* was based upon the Science of the day, and that Science is now obsolete. Its Metaphysic is largely obsolete also. But the greatest of all defects of the *Summa* to modern minds lies in its attitude towards history. The critical treatment of history was unknown either to the orthodox or to the heretics of the Thirteenth Century. More generally we may say that the fatal weakness of this Theology lay in the weakness of its premises. It was believed that the great instrument of human thought was the Syllogism; and the syllogism is merely a means of proving that, if one thing is true, something else must be true also. The Scholastic Theologians show extraordinary sagacity in reconciling contradictions, in clarifying obscurities, in working out the logical consequences of admitted propositions. But there was a fatal weakness about the process by which they got their premises. Except in the case of some fundamental propositions which were—in some cases quite properly—regarded as self-evident, the premises really rested upon a basis of mere authority, whether the authority of Aristotle or of the Bible or of the Church. Why Aristotle should be supposed to be always right, why the Bible should be believed, was a question with which (strange to say) these acute and highly rational thinkers never busied themselves at all. And the consequences of this neglect were all the more serious when we remember the strange system of exegesis which the Middle Ages had inherited from the Alexandrian Fathers.

Can the Schoolmen be of any use to us in spite of these fundamental defects? I think they can.

(1) In the first place, the Schoolmen ordinarily show a magnificent faith in Reason which is not always exhibited by modern theologians, and which is absolutely abhorrent to a large proportion of modern religious people. They believe that God gave us Reason to be used, not (as appears to be thought in some quarters) for the express purpose of deceiving us. These men really grappled with the intellectual difficulties of their age. The great danger to the faith in those days was the newly discovered Aristotle, the Averroism of the Arabic philosophers and their European disciples, and the materialism into which their Averroism tended to degenerate in the minds of the physicians and other crude sceptics of the age. They really grappled with these difficulties and constructed a system of the Universe which satisfied the highest intellects of Europe for some three centuries and longer. Our difficulties are different. To us Darwinism, the higher criticism, historical discovery, are what Aristotle and Averroes were to the men of the Thirteenth Century. If Christianity is to retain its hold upon the thinking and cultivated portion of the world, these difficulties must be grappled with in the spirit, though not by the method, of St. Thomas Aquinas.

(2) Sometimes the Scholastic Theology is valuable as explaining beliefs which we cannot accept; and to understand views which we cannot accept is very often

an essential preliminary to substituting something
better for them. Take, for instance, the case of Transubstantiation. The doctrine grew out of a crude
version of the Platonic doctrine of the reality of
general ideas or Universals which was (with modifi-
cations) also the doctrine of Aristotle. In so far as they
simply asserted the reality of Universal concepts, the
medieval Realists held a doctrine which (as I personally should maintain) is the true solution of the
problem. At all events, it is a doctrine which many
modern philosophers hold. But the tendency of the
scholastic Realist was to think of the Universal as a
sort of semi-material substratum which underlay the
accidents perceived by the senses. The colour, the
taste, the consistency of bread and all the other
qualities which the chemist may discover in it by
analysis were for him mere accidents. These common
qualities were not what made a piece of bread to be
bread; the breadiness of the bread was something
which the senses could not reach; and therefore there
was no contradiction in supposing that all the accidents of this particular piece of bread might remain,
and yet its substance be destroyed. The accidents of
the bread and wine might remain without a substance
for them to inhere in; and therefore no bread might
be there, while the substance of the body and blood of
Christ might be there without any of the accidents of
body and blood. That was what the Medieval mind
understood by the Real Presence, i.e. the presence of
the actual thing. The man who attempts to refute
Transubstantiation by saying that it is refuted by the
evidence of the Senses only shows that he does not
know what the doctrine is. It is a highly philosophical doctrine. It was in its origin an attempt to
present in a refined and intellectually tenable way the
far coarser doctrine of the Real Presence which pre-
vailed in the age just before the formulation of the
doctrine at the Lateran Council of 1215. It is distinctly a philosophical belief; and the reason for aban-

doning it is that it is based upon an extremely bad and untenable philosophy. If this piece of bread is made bread by the common qualities which all bread possesses, if substance is not something which can exist apart from accidents but a relation between accidents or a something which is only intelligible in relation to its accidents, the notion of the substance of one thing disguising itself beneath the accidents of another thing becomes absurd or meaningless.

(3) On certain subjects and within certain limits we may, I believe, still derive positive help from the Schoolmen in the rational presentation of Christian doctrine. On the doctrine of the Incarnation they do not help us much because of their want of historical basis. The men of the Middle Age had little historical knowledge and no historical sense. They had no conception of historical evidence. They had no power of reconstructing the historical background of our Lord's earthly life; and therefore they dealt with the problem of His divine-human nature in a purely abstract, *a priori* way without any serious study of the documents, and generally adopted a theory that humanity was practically swallowed up in the Divinity. The question whether our Lord's knowledge as a man was unlimited was, indeed, freely discussed in the Schools of the Twelfth Century. We have a remarkably interesting treatise on the subject by an Englishman, one Robert of Melun, a famous Parisian Doctor, who became Bishop of Hereford. He contends for the unlimited knowledge; but he does not treat the theory that His knowledge was limited as in any way heretical. It was clear that there were many Scholastics of the time who held that doctrine. Still, from the time of St. Thomas the tendency was to make His knowledge unlimited. In this region we can get no help from the Schoolmen. The Christ of the Schoolmen has no relation to history. He is a creation of the Speculative Reason. It is otherwise when we turn to the doctrine of the Holy Trinity. The

great difficulty which most modern men and women who allow themselves to think freely on such subjects feel about the doctrine of Christ's Divinity is not so much the difficulty of conceiving how God should be revealed in a human personality, as the difficulty of understanding the relation between the Father and the Son before the Incarnation. And so long as this relation is presented to us as a relation between three separate minds, the difficulty of steering a middle course between pure Tritheism and the denial of any Trinity at all in the unity of the Godhead is, I venture to say, insuperable. But that is not the doctrine of St. Augustine. In him we always find the relation between Father, Son, and Holy Spirit compared with the relation between three distinct—eternally distinct —activities of One Divine Mind, never with the relation between three men or other distinct centres of consciousness, as is done by modern theologians such as Canon Mason and Canon Peter Green. He varies a little as to which activities he uses to denote and explain the relation. Sometimes the Father is compared with Memory, by which probably he meant what we should call consciousness, sometimes with Mind; the Son is Intelligence or Wisdom; the Holy Spirit is sometimes Will and sometimes Love (since the Will of God is always a loving will there is no necessary discrepancy between the two). How little St. Augustine uses the word Person in the sense which the word bears either in ordinary modern language or in the language of any modern Philosophy is best seen in his doctrine as to the Holy Spirit. For him the love of the Father for the Son and of the Son for the Father—the mutual love of Father and Son—is the Holy Spirit. Nobody can possibly think of the love of one spiritual being for another as a Person in the modern sense of the term. St. Augustine is quite explicit in affirming that God—the God who is Father, Son, and Holy Spirit—is one Mind (*una mens*), not (as such modern theologians as I have mentioned explicitly teach) three minds as distinct as my mind is from my neighbour's. That is the doctrine of St. Augustine, but it must be admitted that his great treatise, the *De Trinitate*, is full of obscurities, inconsistencies, and unintelligibilities. By the Schoolmen these obscurities are cleared up, and the inconsistencies removed. By Abelard and Peter the Lombard the doctrine of the three Persons is explained to mean that God is Power, Wisdom, and Love. St. Thomas teaches the same doctrine except that in him *Potentia* is replaced by *Principium*. The Father is Power, the Son is the Wisdom or Thought of God, the Holy Spirit is the Love of the Father for the Son, and in Him for all His creatures, and the love of the Son for the Father.

It may be asked what is meant by the love of the Father for the Son if Father and Son are not thought of as distinct Persons in the modern sense of the term? To grasp St. Thomas's thought on this subject it is necessary to bear in mind that for him the Son is not so much the activity of thinking as the object of thought; in his view the Word potentially contains the world, all the human souls that are to be born. The fact therefore that the Father loves the Word does not imply that the Word is a separate mind from the Father. Just as a human being may love the mental picture of the world which he conjures up before his own Mind, so the Father loves the whole world, including the rational beings in it as objects of His own thought. It is more difficult to understand how St. Thomas conceives of the Son or Word as so loving the Father. Perhaps what he meant was that the Incarnate Love and indeed all human beings are eternally present in the thought of God even before their creation in time, that God always knows the love which they will hereafter feel. This is offered only as a tentative explanation: I cannot prove that this was what St. Thomas meant, but I have discovered no better way of explaining one of the greatest dif-

THE SCHOLASTIC THEOLOGY

ficulties in St. Thomas's treatment of the subject.
At all events, whatever St. Thomas may have thought,
it is open to us to adopt it for ourselves. In any case,
the difficulty which we have in interpreting St.
Thomas on this point cannot affect our main conclusion, for St. Thomas thinks God is one spiritual Being,
not three. It is evident that when applied to the distinctions within the Godhead before the Incarnation,
he used Person in a very technical sense quite different
from the sense in which we apply it to this or that
human being. As the very orthodox Schoolman
Richard of St. Victor put it:

" If anyone wants to understand the name of person
under its common and proper acceptance, by no
means let him think that more persons than one can
subsist in the unity of the substance under that ac-
ceptation."

It may be suggested that such questions as these
have no application to the work of the parish priest.
Now, I will not deny that it might be possible to teach
all that it is essential that plain men should know
about God and Christ without raising such problems.
But then you must not teach anything which suggests
these problems. You must avoid altogether such
terms as Person or Substance or the like. But that
is hard to do even if your parishioners are fortunate
enough never to hear the Athanasian Creed. You
would have to suppress the Litany and *Hymns Ancient
and Modern* to keep them in this state of theological
innocence. But if we do use such terms as Person or
Substance, we are bound to do what we can to explain
them and to guard against the almost certain mis-
understandings—alike irrational and unorthodox—
into which they are likely to fall if such terms go unexplained. No doubt with ordinary congregations it
will not be desirable to go very far into such questions.
But I do not see any reason why even children should
not be taught that God is Power, Wisdom, and Love,

M

177

and that that is what is meant by speaking of three persons in One God. There are two questions and answers in the Catechism used by the Roman Catholic Church in England which I should like to see transposed to our own:

"Is there any likeness to the Blessed Trinity in your soul?" "There is this likeness to the Blessed Trinity in my soul: that as in God there are three Persons, so in my soul there are three Powers."

"What are the three powers of my soul?" "The three powers of my soul are my memory, my understanding, and my will."

This language comes from St. Augustine. I should myself prefer St. Thomas's "Power, Wisdom, and Love." But the essential point is that it should be understood that when we speak of the three Persons of the whole Trinity we are using the word Person in a highly technical sense—very remote from that in which we employ it in ordinary life. Unless this is done, the doctrine will mean to children—and to the vast majority of grown-up people—either absolutely nothing, or pure Tritheism. If the Church is to retain any hold over the intellect of the present day, nothing is more essential than that its Monotheism should be beyond dispute. It is one of the chief services of the Scholastic Theology that amid all its complication and intricacy it does make it quite clear that the doctrine of the Holy Trinity does not mean a belief in three Gods. And for that reason among others I could wish—not indeed that our clergy should be brought up upon the Scholastic Theology after the manner of the Roman Seminary, almost to the exclusion of other and more profitable knowledge—but that there should be more generally diffused a little knowledge of the Scholastic Theology considered simply as a chapter in the history of theological thought which is not entirely without value even at the present day. The result of such knowledge would be, I think, not an increased tendency to highly dogmatic teaching, but rather an increased realisation of the fact that much that is commonly taught as though it were something directly revealed from on high is really a product of long centuries of human speculation—as much so as the Philosophy of Hegel or of Bergson. The Scholastic Theology will teach us that, if we insist on raising speculative questions, we must face them as honestly and clearly and thoroughly as the Schoolmen tried to face them, but that the religious teaching that is necessary for the guidance of the individual soul is something very simple and unspeculative. The great defect of much religious teaching at the present day is that it treats as simple and obvious things that are by no means simple and obvious: while it turns into difficult and unintelligible mysteries things that are really very simple and intelligible. The doctrine of the Holy Trinity, as worked out by the Schoolmen, contains much with which even candidates for Holy Orders need not be troubled. But there is no reason why even peasants should not be taught that when the Church asserts that there is only one God, it really means what it says; and that the Trinity which it teaches is simply the Trinity of Power, Wisdom, and Love.

XI

THE ALLEGED IMMANENCE OF GOD

IT is somewhat unfortunate that a recent controversy should have made the " immanence of God " into a sort of watchword of the " New Theology." Under the term " New Theology " seems usually to be included a number of ideas which for more than a generation past have been common ground to Liberal theologians of all denominations—ideas on a variety of subjects which for the most part have this much in common, that they all spring from the rejection of the old-fashioned and the acceptance of the modern or critical attitude towards the Bible. But, though I do not deny that indirectly this changed attitude towards the Bible, and towards dogmas which were supposed to rest upon the authority of the Bible, may have an important influence upon our ideas about the nature of God, it is clear that the adoption of Liberal ideas upon such matters as the Bible, the doctrine of the Atonement, and the interpretation of the ancient Creeds, does not necessarily commit the theologian to the adoption of a side in the old controversy as to the relation of God to the world—the question which is usually stated in the terms " Is God immanent or transcendent? "

Up to a certain point the idea of the Divine Immanence has commended itself to many quite orthodox and conservative theologians. And the opposite view has been strongly advocated by thinkers who are not Christians at all, as well as by those who adopt every possible variety of attitude towards the questions at issue between the more liberal and the more conservative Christian Theology. Consequently I cannot but regard it as somewhat unfortunate that there should be a disposition in some quarters to make the term " immanence of God " into a sort of party rallying-cry of Liberal Theology. In the present article, therefore, I do not wish to be considered to be criti-

cising Mr. Campbell,[1] with the general tone of whose
Theology I feel myself much in sympathy; but to ask,
quite apart from present controversies, whether we
ought to speak of God as immanent, and if the phrase
is to be used at all, what meaning is to be attached to
it?

The popularity of the phrase " Divine Immanence "
would be the less regrettable if it had a fixed, accepted,
and unambiguous meaning. Unfortunately it has
been used to denote a number of opinions which are
much further removed from each other than are the
views of some who employ and of some who strongly
object to such phraseology. Only a few of the meanings with which it is used can be glanced at here. To
the student of Philosophy the word at once suggests
the teaching of Spinoza. Spinoza gives the name
" God " to the one substance which, he believed, underlay all the changes of the Universe. " Matter " and
" Mind " (or " Thought ") were the two attributes
under which this substance manifested itself. To
many people, including some who are really in sympathy with the Christian attitude to the Universe, the
expression " God is everything " (or " everything is
God ") has an edifying and attractive sound, and
such people resent with indignation the suggestion
that Spinoza's view was at bottom atheistic. Technically of course they are right. Spinoza was too acute
a thinker to be imposed upon by a crude Materialism.
He saw how completely the idea of Matter (as known
to us) was made up of terms whose sole meaning lay
in their relation to our consciousness. Consequently he recognised the impossibility of describing
the Ultimate Reality which was the ground alike of
my thinking and of the world as it presents itself to
my thought. He saw too the necessity of ascribing
to the world some kind of unity which could not be
supposed to exist in Matter considered as a mere aggregate of a number of particular things, nor again

[1] R. J. Campbell, *The New Theology* (London, 1907).

in Matter and Mind considered as two totally heterogeneous entities. These and many other of the metaphysical difficulties of Materialism he escaped, or
seemed to escape, by using a neutral term like Substance which could be applied alike to Spirit and to
Matter, and did not necessarily imply either. Technically Spinoza is not a Materialist, for he refused to
commit himself to the doctrine that the world is merely
matter. Spinoza's God is certainly *not* " Matter,"
but neither is it Mind, and therefore we must not
allow ourselves to be imposed upon by the description
of Spinoza in theological language as the " God-in-
toxicated man," nor must we suppose that his God
had anything in common with the God either of
Judaism or Christianity.

Spinoza as little accepted the formula " God is
Matter " as he did the formula " God is Spirit,"
though it may be doubted whether the human mind is
really capable of attributing any meaning to the formula " being which is neither mind nor matter but
which manifests itself in both." The most that can
be really meant by those who adhere to the negative
statement " neither mind nor matter " must be an
" unknowable ground of phenomena," though even
here the old ambiguity breaks out as soon as we attempt to give a meaning to it. " What sort of
ground? " we inevitably ask. Is it a conscious will
or a material thing or a physical force? I doubt
whether anyone really keeps his mind in such a state
of suspense as not secretly to interpret " substance "
either as mind (or something like mind) or as matter
(or something like matter). As to Spinoza himself,
there is every reason to think that he believed in no
mind in the Universe except the mind of man; at
bottom his position was Materialism pure and simple.
But he possessed the metaphysical acuteness not to lay
himself open to the easy refutation which awaits ordinary Materialism at the hands of the metaphysician.
No doubt his view of the Universe did fill him with

an emotion which he chose to express by the term
" intellectual love of God "; but neither " love " nor
" God " implied to him what they imply to ordinary
people. I suspect that at bottom the way in which
the more religiously inclined Spinozist persuades himself that his creed is capable of being made into a
creed which is edifying and stimulating in practice
is by allowing himself to think of his " God " spiritu-
alistically in moments of devotional or ethical feeling;
and then relapsing into a naturalistic way of interpreting his universal Substance the moment he is asked
to expound his creed intellectually.

There are other thinkers, of less metaphysical insight than Spinoza, who seem to mean by "an immanent God" something like the "mind-stuff" of
the late W. K. Clifford. They are men who have no
real appreciation of the metaphysical problem, but
who have just caught a glimpse of the difficulty which
even common-sense discovers in regarding mind as
the mere product of some juxtaposition of material
atoms, and think to evade it by speaking of each piece
of matter as charged with a little mind which under
certain physical conditions condenses and precipitates
itself, as it were, into the conscious minds of men and
animals. It is clear that such theories really make
mind an extremely attenuated sort of matter diffused
throughout space. The crudity of this notion needs no
demonstration. It will impose upon no one who has
gone through an elementary training in Metaphysics.
My only object in mentioning such theories here is to
point out that it is not without ground that both philosophers and common-sense persons are a little suspi-
cious of this language about Immanence when used
by those who profess to be Christian teachers. I am
quite convinced that a great many people who would not
commit themselves to any definite metaphysical theory
really employ the term " immanent " because it seems
to offer a convenient way of conciliating religious
feeling with the supposed requirements of Science.

They are afraid of being thought "Anthropomor-
phic" if they call God a Person or a Will or a Mind;
yet they recognise that we "all believe in a God of
some sort." And so they think to save their reputation for "scientific" thinking by speaking of God (in
their theoretical moments) as a sort of force distri-
buted throughout space, while in their more devotional
or poetic moments they continue to cherish towards
this abstraction the feelings, and to apply to it the
language, which could only be justified by the belief
that God is a Spirit. A moment's reflection will show
that if God is a Spirit, then He is not in Space. And
therefore the term "immanence" can only be applied
to Him by way of metaphor. How far the metaphor
is a desirable or illuminating one it remains for us to
consider.

The intellectual motives, so to speak, which made
the expression "Divine Immanence" acceptable to
those whose attachment to a spiritualistic view of the
Universe is beyond suspicion, are of course intelligible
enough. They want to protest against what is usually
called the Deistic view of the Universe—the idea of
a Divine Clock-maker who originally made the Universe, wound it up, and then let it go of itself. The
term "Deist" is a vague one: in the Eighteenth Century it was applied by the orthodox to thinkers suspected of latitudinarian tendencies, whose opinions
ranged from the moderate orthodoxy of Archbishop
Tillotson to the aggressive anti-Christian fanaticism
of Voltaire; but the typical Deist was one who held
at bottom a mechanical view of the Universe, though
his Philosophy knew of no way of avoiding the necessity of someone to start the machine. He thought of
God as a mere "Creator" who made the world and
then let it alone and took no further interest in it. He
made the laws of Nature, but once made they worked
of themselves. But many of his orthodox opponents
really fell into much the same way of conceiving of
the relation between God and the Universe with one

qualification. They held that the world-clock occasionally got out of order and had to be repaired and
started again by isolated acts of Divine interposition,
consisting in miracles, or Divine communications *ab
extra* guaranteed as such by miracles.

Against this view the supporters of Divine Immanence are no doubt right in protesting. They are right
in insisting that a continuous exercise of the Divine
Intelligence and the Divine Will is as necessary to account for the fall of a stone in accordance with the
law of gravitation or for each stage in the development of the tiniest seed as it would be to account for
the most stupendous violation of the laws of nature
which any theologian has ever believed in. They are
right, too, in thinking of the human mind not as a
mere creation which when once created goes of itself
just like the physical machine with which it is connected; but as having something in common with the
Divine Mind, a reproduction in " a limited mode " of
the Divine Mind and its thoughts. Most attractive
of all does the Immanence theory become when we try
to translate into the thought and language of our time
the traditional language of Creeds and Councils about
the Incarnation of God in Jesus Christ. But the
attractions offered by the phrase should not prevent
our making the effort definitely to ask ourselves what
we really mean by saying that God is " immanent in
the world." When we have done so, we shall be in a
position to decide how much we gain by the use of the
phrase.

It is impossible to be more precise without breaking
up our problem into the three distinctions: (1) the
relation between God and the world; (2) the relation
between God and other minds; (3) the relation between God and the exceptional personality of Christ.
I believe that the mere fact of distinguishing between
the first two of these problems will have done something to clear up our thoughts on the matter. It
seems easy enough to think of God as immanent in the

world, because in the language of common life we are so much accustomed to speaking of the mind as immanent in the body. People forget to ask whether there is any meaning in saying that one mind can be immanent in another mind.

(1) First, then, let us ask whether we can properly speak of God as immanent in the material Universe. Now, in the first place it ought to be pointed out that if the words " immanent in " are to be understood in their natural and obvious sense, they imply a very different theory of the Universe from that which they are often taken to cover. The assertion that " God is immanent " is usually taken as equivalent to the assertion " God is all " or " God is everything "— carrying with it the implication " Nothing exists but what is God." But this is not the obvious meaning of the words. When we say that one thing is or abides in another, we imply that there is a distinction between the two. Popular thought regards the soul as immanent in the body, but it does not regard soul and body as identical. If we are to understand the idea of Divine Immanence as implying that God dwells in matter as the mind dwells in the body, the metaphysician must protest that, strictly speaking, mind cannot occupy space. No doubt there is a sense in which we may say that mind is where it acts, and in that sense there is no harm in saying that the mind is in the body, and that God is in the world, pervading every part of it by His continuous activity. So far the " immanence " doctrine expresses a most important truth. But that is not what is meant by the term as employed by philosophers or philosophic theologians. They mean definitely to say not so much that God is inside the world as that the world is inside God. How far we are justified in such language must depend upon our ultimate metaphysical position. If we are Materialists, the assertion " God is all " is simply another way of saying " There is no God." If we are Spinozists, the assertion becomes (as I have at-

186

tempted to show) practically equivalent to Agnosticism or Naturalism. If we accept the ordinary dualism of the common-sense Theist and believe that Matter is a real thing which might have a being of its own quite independently of its presence to any mind (though as a matter of fact it has actually been created by mind), then to say that " God is all " would mean " God is a name which we give to a collection or aggregate consisting of two different things, Spirit and Matter." The only objection to such a mode of expression is that we now want another word to denote the universal Spirit by which the material world was created and sustained. It would therefore be more convenient and natural to reserve the word for the creative and sustaining Spirit, and to call the aggregate (Matter plus Spirit) " the Universe."

And this is what is actually done by Theology when it rejects Idealism. The identification of God with the material world (when not made in the sense of Spinozism) is usually associated with the idealistic doctrine that Matter has no independent existence; that in truth all that has real existence is Spirit; that what we call matter is simply the object or thought or experience of mind. I must not here attempt an argument in favour of Idealism nor must I stay to distinguish between the various kinds of Idealism. I will merely say that upon the idealistic view of the Universe (which I hold myself) there is no objection to saying that Matter is not outside God—or even part of God's nature—only on two understandings.

In the first place, we must beware of being misled by the spatial associations of " inside " and " outside," and recognise distinctly that we are employing metaphor. God does not occupy space, and therefore He is not diffused throughout the world. It is true to say that space and the spatial world is " in " God, but it is " in " Him as a man is in his thought and other conscious experience, not in the sense in which one material may be in another.

And, secondly, the metaphysical assertion that the world is the thought of God, or in more poetic language that Nature is " the robe of God," and the like, must not be understood to mean that God has no thought except the world—still less that the world is thought without a thinker. The philosopher whose influence has contributed most to the popularity of such phraseology is of course Hegel. Yet nobody has ever succeeded in discovering what Hegel's notion of God was. He asserts over and over again that God is only Spirit; but it is not clear how far he really believed that there is any conscious thought or will in the Universe except the consciousness of man. Among the disciples who repeat his formula it is certain that the most opposite meanings are attached to it; and all of them can find support in some portion of their master's voluminous writings. There are those who (though in their formal writings they employ edifying language which imposes upon the simple-minded) privately and occasionally ridicule the idea that " the Absolute " has any consciousness except the limited and perishable consciousness of individual men or of whatever other such organisms may inhabit other planets; while much the same language is employed by High Anglicans, who are attracted by the facilities which Hegelian formulae supply for a philosophical presentation of a rather tritheistic Trinitarianism, and by others whose serious attachment to Theism cannot be doubted. And all alike believe themselves to be simply expounding the thought of their great Master. What Hegel meant, whether he knew what he meant, and whether he really meant to say what he thought, what were his motives for not wishing to say what he thought, or why (if he did wish to say what he thought) he did not succeed in making his meaning unambiguous—these and many other questions which arise in this connection I must leave undetermined. I only wish to call attention to the fact that the existence of an important philosophical school in England and

America (for there are no Hegelians in Germany) which uses the language of "immanence" in senses varying from pure Naturalism to High Anglicanism may excuse the attitude of suspicion on the part of both common-sense persons and of philosophers not in sympathy with Hegelianism towards Christian theologians or ecclesiastics who employ the same language.

But on the understandings that I have intimated, there is no objection to saying that the world is not outside God, even though the expression is so ambiguous that it is best avoided. We do not commonly think of a person's thoughts as being the person himself, though on reflection we do not deny that the thoughts have no existence outside the person. For those who do not want to identify Nature with God, who believe that God is a Consciousness, a Mind, a Will, it will surely be enough to assert that the world is thought by and willed by God, without continually indulging in language which may be so easily extended to cover the idea that there is no God but an unconscious Nature which somehow gives birth to conscious animals. Once again there is no harm in saying " Nature or the world is in God," still less in saying " God is immanent in Nature," with its distinct implication that God and Nature are distinguishable from each other. It is only when we come to the application of such phraseology to the relation between God and finite spirits that objections to the phrase become serious both from the point of view of pure metaphysical truth and from that of practical Religion and Morality.

(2) The idea that every human being is a part of God is one very widely diffused among professed philosophers, and when clothed in the language of poetry or edification is one which finds a ready acceptance with a certain class of minds not specially conversant with technical metaphysics. Nevertheless I venture to assert that the idea is one which will not

stand serious examination. Of course, if God be first
defined as " the Ultimate Reality " or " the Absolute "
or " the Infinite," it is easy to show that individual
minds, if, and in so far as, they are real at all must
be parts of the Ultimate Reality, the Absolute, or the
Infinite. And there are of course philosophers who
in maintaining that we are parts of God mean simply
that God is a name for the sum of individual minds.
Theirs is a position which I cannot now stop to examine. I am approaching the subject from the point
of view of those who are not satisfied by such a conception of God, who believe that God is a conscious
Spirit who wills, thinks, feels, or at least has a consciousness which can only be understood by us as
something analogous to the experiences which we call
willing, thinking, and feeling in ourselves. From this
point of view the question is whether any meaning
can be attached to the assertion that the Divine Mind
includes a number of different consciousnesses. The
contention that such an inclusion is unmeaning and
unthinkable is generally met with a shrug of the
shoulders and a silence suggesting a profound sense
of conscious philosophical superiority, or (if the discussion is conducted on religious rather than metaphysical lines) with the solemn remark that the
religious position is only intelligible to the religious.
It is no doubt always impossible to argue against those
who say that in their inner consciousness they see with
perfect distinctness that propositions which seem
mutually contradictory to others are nevertheless perfectly reconcilable to them, while they admit their
total inability to explain in human language how they
have succeeded in " transcending the difference " between them. I can only appeal to the intelligence of
my readers. To me it appears quite clear—clearer
than almost any other truth in the whole universe of
knowledge—that every moment of consciousness is
in its own nature absolutely unique. My thoughts,
feelings, emotions, are for ever mine and not
190

another's; or rather (to avoid all difficult questions about the nature of Personality) I would say, they are for ever themselves and not anything else. Another person may feel or think what I feel or think; but then there are two thoughts or feelings, not one. Even my own knowledge of them, after they are gone, is not the same feeling and thought which I once experienced.

No doubt I may make abstraction of the fact that the thought or the feeling is mine. I may say that what I think and feel is *the same* as what the other person thinks and feels; but abstractions are not realities. Of course when I and another person feel alike, the feelings are the same when I have made abstraction of that in them which is different. The *content* of the thought or of the feeling is the same: but content means some universal character which, though it is undoubtedly part of reality, has no real existence except in the individual beings in which it is manifested or realised. I may know that another suffers pain or experiences pleasure, but the knowledge of a pain or a pleasure is a very different thing from the pain or pleasure itself. However completely therefore God may know what human beings think or feel, however completely similar thoughts or feelings may form part of His consciousness, that does not justify me in saying that my thought or feeling is a part of God. If by God is meant a consciousness and if by myself is meant another consciousness, my Self cannot be a part of God: in that sense God is not the all. The philosophic " Absolute " or " Ultimate Reality " no doubt includes me; but the philosophic Absolute is not what the religious consciousness means by God. Mystics have no doubt aspired to a union with God in which personality or selfhood is lost. I will not attempt now to examine the reasonableness or the piety of such an aspiration. I will only point out that the very fact that it was to them an object of aspiration shows that they believed that at one time such an identity did not exist, and they have always very emphatically held that the way to it was steep and difficult and the goal was one which few can reach. Such experiences therefore supply no evidence in favour of the idea that every human and animal consciousness is a part of God. The idea seems at bottom to arise from that fertile source of philosophic error—the abuse of spatial metaphor. Chinese boxes can be what they are and yet be included in one another: such a relation is quite unintelligible when applied to the totally different case of minds. To crude thinkers the idea no doubt seems intelligible because they conceive of minds as existences occupying space; but even philosophers who cannot be accused of such an obvious absurdity as this do not seem to me to have altogether escaped the misleading influence of the spatial analogy. We are no doubt obliged to employ that analogy if we are to think or speak about minds at all, but that does not justify us in assuming that everything that is true of a whole composed of parts in space is true also of a whole when parts are minds.

I have no doubt that by many the formulae " God is all " and the like are used without the least intention of suggesting that my actual thoughts, feelings, and volitions are a part of what God thinks, feels, and wills. By the " ego " which is part of God they do not mean actual moments of conscious experience, but the real thing which is the source or ground or cause of those successive moments of consciousness. Yet such a view may be maintained in a form which annihilates the individual self implied in our consciousness, and therewith the possibility of real self-determination, responsibility, morality. The existence of the permanent individual self is indeed as much an immediate datum of consciousness as the existence of its successive conscious states. If all that is meant is that the individual self is not an " independent soul," i.e. that it has the ground alike of its beginning and of its continued existence from moment to moment in an existence larger than itself, then this assertion is unobjectionable. We *may*, therefore, if we please, talk of a unity of substance underlying the difference between God and man, and between one individual mind and another; or of a single mind as the ground or cause of all that is. We may further insist, and with good reason, that the individual selves must not be treated as arbitrary products of God's activity, as if made by His fiat to be something quite unlike Himself and with thoughts and ideas quite unlike His own. We may in fact reasonably infer that the consciousness which God communicates to His creatures is like His own, in proportion to the degree of their capacity. Even a mind that is merely conscious of pleasure and pain must have something in it like the consciousness of God. And in the higher achievements of the human mind we may reasonably discern a gradual revelation of the world as God thinks it, since all knowledge is from the idealistic point of view a kind of Revelation. Still more truth and importance is there in this view of the relation between Divine and human knowledge when we come to man's knowledge of the moral ideal and his knowledge of God.

The idea of the Divine Immanence would be harmless enough if it meant merely to assert that there is a certain communication of Divine knowledge to the human mind, and the consequent possibility in moral and religious experience of a real communion between God and man. Human minds may well enough be spoken of in Green's language as " reproductions " of the Universal Self-consciousness and in the language of an older Philosophy as " emanations " or " sparks " of the Divine mind. But there is nothing in all this to justify the idea that the human consciousness is part of God. The reproduction of a statue is not identical with its model; the emanation is not identical with that from which it was an emanation; the spark when once it has become a spark is no longer part of the parent fire. When once it is admitted that

N   193

the actual human consciousness is not the same as
God's or part of it, we cannot justify the statement
" God is all." A Divine mind is not in the strict
philosophical language the Infinite, if there is something which it is not. Doubtless for the Theist nothing has an independent, self-sufficient existence apart
from God; in that sense we may if we like speak of
God as the Infinite. But the word is one without
which we could get on just as well. Once again, the
misleading associations of spatial metaphor come in.
If we refuse to call God the Infinite, we shall inevitably
be asked whether He is finite; and if we say that He
is, we shall be supposed to believe in some eternally
co-existent entity spatially outside Him, and resisting
His activities. " Infinite " and " finite " had better be
reserved for space and time, which are not themselves
existences independent of what is in space and time.

For many minds there is something edifying and
consoling in the idea that the human mind is literally
a part of the Divine. When a man confines his attention to saints and heroes, that may possibly be the
case; and no doubt the suggestion that he is himself
a part of the Divine mind may be welcome enough to
the natural vanity of very ordinary characters. But
the attractiveness of this idea must surely disappear
if it is duly remembered that, according to the theory,
the saint cannot be regarded as a part of God in any
other sense or degree than Caesar Borgia or the biggest historical scoundrel that has not yet been white-
washed by some episcopal or other historian is a part
of God. For, be it remembered, when we think of the
relation between man and God as the relation of part
to whole, we have no right to introduce differences of
degree. When the human mind is thought of as a
revelation, or emanation, or reproduction of God, we
may reasonably introduce such differences. We
may regard the human mind as reproducing or revealing God's nature more truly and fully than an animal,
the educated European more adequately than the savage,

194

the men of high ideals more than the men of lower
ones, the man that lives up to his ideals more than the
man who falls short of them.   But if it is a question
of whole and part, we have no right to such distinctions: we might no doubt talk about a smaller and a
larger part.   But surely the shock that the reverent
mind naturally experiences on being told that some
monster of iniquity—not some part or aspect of him,
but the whole man just as he is with all his vices and
iniquities—is wholly and literally part of God, will not
be much mitigated by saying that he is only a little part
of Him.   And after all, if the question is merely one
of magnitude, the very good are probably in a minority,
and have therefore less right to be taken as representing or revealing the true nature of God than the bad
and the mediocre.   To regard every soul as equally
part of God puts an end to the possibility of regarding
God as a moral being.

And the immoral deductions which may be made
from the position under discussion are no mere speculative possibilities.   There are not wanting at the
present moment philosophers who are prepared to
follow out the logic of their own pantheism.   They
recognise that every soul is equally a part of God, and
therefore has as much right as any other to be taken
as revealing the character of the Absolute or Whole
of which they are parts or (as some prefer to put it)
"appearances."   If so, good and evil must be from
the point of the whole equally essential to the perfection or good of the whole.   The idea that the good
ought to be and the bad ought not to be suppressed
must be put down to a mere error or prejudice due to
the limitations of human thought.   Pages have been
written in praise of wickedness no less eloquent than
any of those which our Hegelianising divines have
penned in praise of virtue.

It is not therefore without ground that conservative theologians insist upon the tendency of a pan-
theising theology to lower our practical estimate of

sin and moral evil. After all, it needs no very elaborate demonstration to show that if all souls are equally part of God, God cannot be an object of moral reverence. A Religion that is based on such a Theology must be a Religion that frankly takes leave of Ethics. The real thinkers who have adopted this kind of position are not slow to admit the deduction. They are fond of praising Religion and depreciating morality just because of the alleged sublime indifference of Religion to Morality. To the religious man, we are told, nothing exists but what ought to exist. From his point of view all that is, is good, because all is equally part of the will of God: evil is merely apparent.

I do not doubt that there have been Christian mystics who, in the extravagances of ecstasy, have adopted language which really does invite this kind of Antinomianism or Immoralism. But as a rule the religious minds believed that God is good, and that evil exists in spite of His will. At all events, the attitude of the "supermoral" religious man is fundamentally irreconcilable with the attitude of Jesus of Nazareth and from that generally prevalent among the professors of the Religion which calls itself by His name. The theologians who have picked up a Philosophy that does not suit them are of course quite innocent of any such anti-ethical intentions. They have merely fallen into the mistake of attempting to base a Christian Philosophy upon a misunderstood Hegel, when they would have found a better foundation for their practical faith in Leibniz or Lotze or James Ward. But their Philosophy cannot be pronounced Christian because they are blind to its true drift, nor is their teaching rendered really innocuous because something like it may occasionally be heard from the lips of a writer in *Lux Mundi* or from the pulpit of the City Temple.

I must be allowed to point out another consequence of the view which I am examining. I will not say

that that view is absolutely fatal to the idea of personal Immortality. But the whole drift of that line
of thought is against any such Eschatology; and the
real thinkers who have adopted it are generally aware
of this tendency. If everything that separates man
from his fellows or from God or produces the appearance of such a separation is to be treated as a limitation, a mere appearance, possibly a delusive appearance, then the more optimistic our view of the future
of our race, the more desirable and probable will it
appear that these limitations will disappear, and that
the individual man will be absorbed back into the All
from which he came, and to which (in spite of the
delusive sense of personality) he has never ceased to
belong. Such has been the view of both Brahminism
and Buddhism; though the anti-ethical tendency of
such a theory is mitigated in those religions by the
doctrine of transmigration which interposes a multi-
tude of lives—lives dependent for their character upon
present conduct—between the individual's present
stage of existence and his ultimate absorption into an
All which is generally thought of as unconscious.
For reasons which need hardly be pointed out, this
idea of transmigration is not very likely to appeal to
modern thinkers who reject the idea of Immortality.
The absorption into the Infinite which they contemplate is likely with them to mean an immediate cessa-
tion of consciousness after death. The real thinkers
who use this language mean what it means: they reject—generally with scorn and indignation—the idea
that such a progress can reinforce the sense of personal responsibility, in that it has everything in
common with the old hopes and fears which have
done so much in the past to emphasise the cosmic
importance of individual conduct. It is in vain for
Christian preachers to think that they can talk about
a continuance of personal life side by side with the
doctrine of absorption into the Infinite. The language
by which they attempt thus to fuse perfectly irrecon-

cilable views of the Universe generally involves obvious self-contradiction.

If I am to exist after death, it is meaningless to talk about the absorption into the Infinite; if I am to be absorbed into the Infinite, it is meaningless to speak about *my* continued existence. The continued existence of a Being which will be no longer " I " cannot be to me a subject of any more interest than the continued existence of future generations whom I have not known; and if good and bad conduct are alike followed by such absorption, the prospect of such an existence can do nothing to reinforce the importance of personal Morality. To these considerations I may add the fact that the only rational ground for the belief in personal Immortality is to be found in the dictates of the Moral Consciousness. It is because the Moral Consciousness declares that the wages of goodness *ought* not to be dust that it becomes difficult to believe that in a mind-governed Universe it can virtually be so. But a Philosophy which represents the good man and the bad as equally parts of a single all-embracing Being tends to make the consciousness of a final and ultimate authority in the moral faculty a delusion. A Philosophy which is based upon the primacy of the Practical Reason cannot admit that we can attribute to God the moral character of Caesar Borgia in the same sense and with the same truth that we can regard the character of the best man whose life history records, as a revelation of His nature.

(3) The glance that I have bestowed upon the religious and ethical consequences of the " Immanence " doctrine naturally leads up to the third division of our subject. The attraction which the formula " Divine Immanence " exercises upon the philosophic theologian is largely due to the fact that it facilitates a rational explanation of the Catholic doctrine of the Incarnation. It is widely felt by reasonable theologians that if Christ is not to be made a mere

psychological portent—utterly unintelligible to the human mind, utterly irreconcilable with the results of a critical study of His life and character—any philosophical defence of His Divinity must begin by presupposing that what is true in an exceptional and unique degree of Christ is true to some extent and in some measure of the relation of all human nature to God. With this line of thought I am myself in the fullest sympathy. But I would suggest that the " Immanence " doctrine is not really necessary in order to allow the Christian theologian to avail himself of it. It is no doubt tempting to the man who wants to reconcile an apparently uncompromising orthodoxy with a profoundly philosophical position; for it enables him to say without any qualification or hesitation " Christ is God." I will not insist much upon the fact that such a position is not technically orthodox, since it either denies the real humanity of Christ or else asserts that the human nature of Christ is God. But I will endeavour to point out that such a defence of the " Incarnation " doctrine really gives up all that makes it of religious and ethical importance to assert it. If I assert Christ is God, and then go on to assert " In the same sense it is equally true that Judas Iscariot was God," clearly I have given up all that gives a religious value to the doctrine. On pantheistic premises, as I have endeavoured to point out. there is no ground for a doctrine of degrees of divinity in men. The real value of the doctrine of Christ's Divinity is in its authorising us to think of God in the light of the moral ideal He taught and the character He exhibited in the historical Christ. This we can do without saying that the human Jesus was a part of God. Surely it is enough to say that while all humanity reveals in its measure and degree the character of God, humanity at its highest is the fullest revelation of God that the human mind can understand; and that humanity, in its moral and religious aspect, attained its highest level in the historical Christ.

I am not very solicitous to defend the technical orthodoxy of this representation, but I believe it could be done. Men in the Twentieth Century cannot think exactly as men in the Third or the Fifth Century thought. The most orthodox view of the Incarnation that is held by any modern scholar who knows what Philosophy and Criticism mean is not really the same as the view of Athanasius or Augustine, but it may be a quite legitimate development of it. And I believe that what I have said does really contain the core of what the old theologians meant by the Divinity of Christ, though they no doubt often drew inferences from it—inferences about the unlimited miraculous power and unlimited intellectual knowledge of Christ —which the modern theologian will not draw. In a more elaborate treatment of this matter I should call attention to the fact that the doctrine of two natures in Christ saves the doctrine of Divine Immanence from either of the two opposite exaggerations to which it is liable. By asserting that the human nature of Christ is not identical with the Divine, it emphasises the fact that there is something in Christ the man (as in every other man) which is not God, or something (if we wish to be technically correct, as Divine predicates may be applied to it) which is God only in virtue of its unity with the Divine nature. By asserting that it is the Logos or Wisdom dwelling or revealing itself in Him which is Divine, it makes it clear that, though God is revealed in humanity, it is Christ in whose character and teaching the Divine nature has been most conspicuously revealed: and it makes it plain that God is not *merely* the sum of the minds to whom He communicates some of His own nature and His own knowledge.

Leaving the technical distinctions aside, I will only insist once more that the idea of God's Immanence in Humanity cannot be regarded as a metaphysically, and still less as a religiously or ethically, valuable doctrine unless it be made plain (i) that this Immanence does not make the actual thoughts, feelings, and volitions of human beings identical with the Divine consciousness or any part of it; (ii) that that revelation or reproduction of the Divine consciousness which does take place in human and other minds—sub-human or (it may be) higher than human—is a matter of degree, and that it reaches its highest point in that moral consciousness which forbids us to say that a criminal is as divine as a saint. To speak of God as immanent in the historic Christ is the least objectionable application of the phrase, just because it is the least likely to involve the obscuring of these important truths. The very fact that God is regarded as immanent in Christ in a way different from that in which He was present in other men implies that we cannot with equal truth say that God was immanent in a Borgia or in a Buonaparte. Once more I may insist that if the term " immanent in " is to be taken with any strictness, it implies that there was something in which God was immanent and with which therefore He was not identical. So long as the phrase be understood thus strictly, it cannot be regarded as convertible with what I venture to call the meaningless and, properly speaking (however excellent the intentions of its supporters), blasphemous assertion " God is all." But, inasmuch as the phrase " Divine Immanence " is constantly used in this sense, it would be well for those who do not sympathise with such pantheistic tendencies to employ it with caution and reserve. Perhaps as a rule it had better be avoided altogether; and the truth which it contains be expressed, as I have endeavoured to show that it can perfectly well be expressed, in other and less ambiguous language.

XII

THE METAPHYSIC OF MR. F. H. BRADLEY [1]

THE critical period for great literary reputations is the generation after that for which the authors wrote or by which they were first appreciated. The generalisation holds as much in regard to professional Philosophy as in more popular branches of literature —only that with philosophical reputations the generations are short and succeed each other with great rapidity. In Philosophy the craving for something new is even keener than in literature; a Philosophy that has to any extent become official soon becomes an object of suspicion to the questioning spirits. The philosophical reputation of Mr. Bradley has, it would appear, reached this stage. His is no longer the last word in Philosophy. He has outlived the period in which young and enthusiastic disciples were disposed to set down all the philosophies that preceded his, except the great philosophical classics, as matters of merely historical interest. It is not yet certain that he will be treated as himself belonging to those classics. That period can hardly be reached till his reputation has spread beyond the limits of the English-speaking world, for in England the road to eminence is to be talked about in other countries; and English philosophical reputations are slow to attract the attention of continental thinkers. This process has only just begun in the case of Mr. Bradley. Meanwhile there is a danger that the importance of his works should be unduly overshadowed by that of writers who have succeeded in administering more recent and still more sensational shocks to traditional modes of thought. That danger is all the greater since Mr. Bradley's reputation was always an esoteric one. It has never reached the greater public—even the public of highly cultivated persons outside the

[1] A paper read before the British Academy, June 5, 1912. Reprinted from the *Proceedings of the British Academy*, vol. V.

circle of those who have at least studied Philosophy
a little in their youth: while the philosophies which
are now absorbing most attention even among professional students of the subject are philosophies which
—whether that be regarded as a merit or a defect—
are particularly adapted to attract to themselves a
measure of attention in the world of religious thought
and of general literature. I hope the present moment
will not be an unfavourable one for attempting an
impartial examination of Mr. Bradley's metaphysical
position.

As this paper will be chiefly critical, I should like
to begin by saying that I am one of those who do
place Mr. Bradley among the classics of Philosophy.
When *Appearance and Reality* came out, Dr. Edward
Caird said that it was the greatest thing since Kant.
I should like respectfully to subscribe that dictum at
least in the form " there has been nothing greater
since Kant." It is not likely, indeed, that Mr. Bradley's actual reputation will ever place him quite in
this position. The greatest and most enduring philosophical reputations will always be those of men who
have not merely offered a new solution of the technical problems of Philosophy but have expounded
some new and 'characteristic attitude towards life.
Mr. Bradley—apart from a few *obiter dicta* which
in all spheres except the religious are for the most
part of an extremely conservative cast—has touched
little on practical questions. Perhaps therefore his
writings will never become quite as classical as they
deserve to be. But just because I regard Mr. Bradley as a classic, I shall venture to handle him with
the freedom which we all employ towards the great
names of Philosophy. One is almost tempted to say
that the greatest thinkers are just those who have
made the greatest mistakes. We are all agreed that
there are huge inconsistencies in Kant: much the same
thing is beginning at least to be whispered about
Hegel; and yet we do not cease to regard Kant or

even Hegel as great men. I trust therefore that, if I venture to point out similar inconsistencies in Mr. Bradley, I shall not be supposed to be wanting in respectful admiration for his work. I need not say that it is only in the most inadequate way that in such a paper as this I can attempt an examination even of one or two central points in his elaborate construction—if the word can be applied to a system which is so much more destructive than constructive. A full examination of *Appearance and Reality* would demand a work at least as long.

If criticism must be brief, exposition must be briefer. And yet, even before an audience whose adequate acquaintance with the book may be pre-supposed, I can hardly begin to criticise without some slight attempt to state the positions I am attacking—if only for the purpose of indicating incidentally what are the elements of Mr. Bradley's thought which I regard as constituting his real philosophical importance.

Appearance and Reality may be described as the work of an inquirer in search of Reality. The first and most obvious suggestion which would occur to the plain man in search of the real is " Things are real." An examination of what we mean by things shows that no *thing,* taken by itself, can be real. I need not recapitulate the ordinary idealistic argument by which it is shown that all that we mean by a thing is unintelligible apart from Mind. Secondary qualities are obviously constituted by feeling or perception, 'or by a content which is ultimately derivable from perception. Even " Common-sense " does not suppose that things would be coloured if there were no one to see them, or scented if there were no one to smell them. Primary qualities are equally relative to Mind: for extension, taken apart from something which is extended, is a mere abstraction; and that something which is extended is always something given in immediate perception. In a world in which there were no perception and no percipients, there would be nothing to be extended. The force and clearness with which Mr. Bradley has insisted upon this point constitutes the most original feature in his re-statement of the case for Idealism. Moreover, when we do make the abstraction of extension from the extended, we find that extension so considered consists in relations, and relations by themselves are unintelligible without qualities. Here Mr. Bradley cannot quite use the argument, commonly employed by Idealists, that, while relations—at least the particular relations which enter into the constitution of space and of things in space—are nothing apart from a mind that apprehends the relation, they become fully intelligible when looked at in their due connection with Mind: for according to him the relation between relations and that which is related is ultimately unintelligible. But at all events the fact that spatial relations cannot be thought of as existing by themselves is enough to show that neither the spatial relations themselves nor things in space can be the reality of which we are in search; for relations imply qualities, and the qualities have been shown to exist only for mind.

I will return to Mr. Bradley's peculiar view about the unintelligibility of relations hereafter. As to his general polemic against the notion that matter is real, I need not dwell further upon a line of argument which Mr. Bradley shares with all Idealists. I will only say, in view of recent revivals of the naïvest form of what we used to have the audacity to call naïve Realism, that to me one great value of Mr. Bradley's teaching consists in this—that he is the most thoroughly convinced and the most convincing, I venture to think the most irrefutable, of Idealists. In Mr. Bradley we have an Idealist who is not afraid or ashamed of Idealism. Mr. Bradley is not a " soft Idealist " who, after disposing of Materialism by arguments borrowed from Berkeley or Kant, suddenly, when faced with the difficulties of his own tradition and its antagonism to so-called Common-sense, turns round and condemns under the name of " subjective Idealism " the inevitable inference " if nature does not exist apart from Mind, then nothing really exists but Mind and what is *for* mind." Mr. Bradley is a genuine, hard, impenitent Idealist, who over and over again asserts as his fundamental formula " There is but one Reality, and its being consists in experience." [1] Experience, be it observed, not (with Berkeley) " ideas," used practically in the sense of feelings, or (with Hegel) mere " thought." Mr. Bradley recognises that all thought involves abstraction— abstraction from an experience which always is, or includes, feeling. He further differentiates himself from much traditional Hegelianism by recognising the existence of a distinct side of human experience called " willing " which can, quite as little as feeling, be reduced to a mere kind of thinking, unless thinking is to be used in a completely non-natural sense which leaves us without a word to denote what ordinary people call thinking. Hence Mr. Bradley's preference for the most comprehensive term that we can possibly apply to conscious life—experience. It turns out then as the result of examination that matter, as we know it, can always be analysed away into a form of conscious experience. Consequently matter, understood as a thing existing apart from mind, cannot be real.

But if matter be not real, because in ultimate analysis it turns out to be a mere accident of mind, why should not mind itself be the reality of which we are in search? By mind let us first understand the individual human self as we know it. It is obvious that such a self cannot be the real in the sense of the only reality: for such selves have a beginning, and only a small part of the world which Science reveals to us enters into the actual experience of any particular self; and when it does enter into it, it enters

[1] *Appearance and Reality,* p. 455. Cf. pp. 146-7.

it in a way which implies that such entrance into an individual experience does not constitute the sole existence that the world can claim. We are bound to infer that things existed before we were born; the continual advance of our knowledge implies that there must be some existent things of which no human self has at present the smallest suspicion, and so on. But Mr. Bradley is not content with asserting that neither any individual self nor all the selves put together are the Reality. He will not admit that they are real at all, or any part of the Reality. And here it becomes necessary to allude to a peculiar feature of Mr. Bradley's nomenclature or rather, we ought to say, of his thought. His conception of " the real " is that it is that which is not in relation—that which is what it is wholly in and by itself, so that nothing outside it is necessary to maintain or to complete its being.[1] Sometimes the statement is varied by saying that " the real is individual," [2] or (what will seem to most of us to introduce a wholly heterogeneous and a purely ethical conception) the real is " the perfect." [3] This will strike most people on the face of it as a very arbitrary conception of the real. Mr. Bradley, in fact, begins by assuming that in saying something is real we mean that is the whole of Reality. This position rests upon the further allegation—that the real cannot contradict itself; Non-contradiction is the test of reality [4]; and relation always does involve contradiction. But before examining Mr. Bradley's proof of this startling position, I must briefly trace its consequences.

If to be out of relation is the essence of Reality, it is clear that the individual self cannot be real. For if the object of knowledge cannot be regarded as real apart from the subject, equally little can we find in the subject taken apart from the object an entity which owes nothing of its being to its relations to any

[1] Ibid., pp. 129, 136-7, 140-3.
[2] Ibid., p. 140. [3] Ibid., pp. 243-5. [4] Ibid., p. 136.

other being. The self always reveals itself to us in the act of thinking something, and it distinguishes itself from that something. Moreover, the self is not only made what it is by relation to the object, but by relation to other selves. We have failed to find the reality that we want in the self—taken in any of the numerous senses in which the term self may be and actually is used. But can we not find such a reality in a self free from the limitations of the self as we know it—such a Self as the God of theistic Religion is supposed to be? To such a position Mr. Bradley objects that such a Mind must still be conceived of as related to the objects of His own knowledge whether these objects are looked upon simply as inevitable objects of thought existing in and for Him but independently of His will, or whether they are treated as caused or created by the Mind which knows them. And then, moreover, according to the ordinary theistic conception, the other selves—of men and animals—are regarded as being outside this divine Mind, and so related to that Mind: and yet those relations necessarily form part of the nature of the divine Mind itself. Once again we have relation: and so not Reality.

We might seem to reach a more tenable position if we adopted—if not *the* Hegelian position—at least one version of that position very common among Hegelians, and say that the divine Mind must be thought of as including all other minds, and also as including the objects of its knowledge. We might then suppose that the All is real, that in the one comprehensive Mind or Spirit which includes, and is, all other and lesser minds we have found the one sole, absolute Reality. But this will not satisfy Mr. Bradley's demand for unrelatedness. For, though we have got rid of external relations, we have not got rid of internal relations. So long as we think of the All as a whole consisting of parts—including within itself subject + object, this self + that self, or even this self as within or a part of that self, we are still conceiving of our reality as made up of inter-related parts or elements: and to be involved in relation is, according to his definition, to be unreal. Nothing can be real but the whole; and even the whole is not real, so long as it is considered as a whole, a collection, a plurality of parts.

Are we then frankly to admit that Reality does not exist at all? That would be unthinkable and even self-contradictory. In calling some things unreal or appearance, we imply that there must be a Real with which such unrealities can be contrasted. Appearance is only intelligible as an appearance *of* the Real. To think of something as *merely* an appearance is to think of it as ultimately adjectival: and the adjective implies a substantive. If there were no reality, there could be no appearance: of the appearances we are immediately conscious; and their existence as appearances is consequently undeniable. Hence we must say, not that the All or the Whole as such *is* the real, but that the real is that which underlies all appearances, which is revealed more or less adequately, more or less inadequately, in all appearance. It is the whole only if we think of the whole as including the parts otherwise than by way of relation, as a whole which swallows up the parts so completely that all relation disappears, and they cease to be even parts. Knowledge of this Reality—this Absolute, as Mr. Bradley delights to call it—we can never obtain, for to know the Absolute at once implies that distinction between knower and known which cannot belong to the real. To know the Absolute I should have to *be* the Absolute. And even then I could not know myself, for even in self-knowledge a relation breaks out again—the fatal Dualism which we want to get rid of; the distinction between knower and known, between part and whole, which implies a relation between them.

This thesis—that Reality cannot be fully known or

o

thought—is further defended by an elaborate attempt
to show that all the categories of our thought imply incoherences or contradictions, inconsistencies which we
cannot suppose to belong to Reality. This in fact
is the topic with which the greater part of the book
is occupied. I must be content with noticing only
one or two counts in this indictment against knowledge.

(1) In the first place all knowing, as *we* know—all
judging—implies abstracting. It consists in the application of abstract universals to a logical subject. Yet this
abstract universal does not as such exist except in my
head. The "green in general" which I predicate of the
grass is a green which no eye has ever seen. Nobody ever saw a "green in general"—which was
neither light-green nor dark-green, neither bright nor
dull, neither distinct nor indistinct. In immediate
perception I am, indeed, in close and immediate contact with Reality, but the moment I begin to think,
I in a sense get away from Reality, for I begin making abstract universals which leave out so much of
the actual fact as it is in perception. And yet all
Science implies this getting away from Reality, this
dealing with abstract universals. In knowledge we
are as it were dealing with counters which are in a
sense fictions—though they stand for, and are ex-
changeable with and facilitate our relations with
actual Reality. And yet on the other hand so long
as we merely feel and do not think, we have no knowledge. In actual perception this disruption between
subject and predicate has not yet taken place. All
predication consists in putting asunder what Reality
has conjoined. From the nature of the case, therefore, Reality cannot be fully known: and, wherever
we do not know fully, we are always liable to error—
we do not and cannot know how much error. Hence
we are involved in this dilemma. If we knew the
Absolute, what we knew could not be real just because
it is the object of knowledge: in proportion as our

experience becomes more real, the further it gets away from knowledge. The nearer to Reality, the further from truth: the more truth, the less Reality. Truth, in other words, cannot be perfectly true: if it were perfectly true, it would no longer be truth. Reality can never be known: directly it becomes known, it is no longer Reality.

(2) The most fundamental of all Mr. Bradley's alleged self-contradictions in our knowledge is connected with the category of Relation. It is, as I have already said, upon the allegation that the relative is the self-contradictory that his whole theory of the absolute Reality turns. All our knowledge is found on analysis to consist of feeling, or a content derived from feeling, and relation. We never have the one without the other—feelings without relation or relations without feeling. Each is unintelligible without the other: and yet the relation between them is itself unintelligible. Directly we try to think of the relation between the relation and that which is related, we find that it implies a further relation between them—which gives rise to the problem, what is the relation between this relation and the relation between the relation and the related, and so on *ad infinitum*. The category of Relation involves a *regressus ad infinitum,* which cannot be thought of as belonging to Reality. Our thought, all thought as such, is therefore for ever incapable of getting itself into contact with the real world as it is.

(3) The other categories of our thought—cause and effect, substance and accident, quantity and quality—are likewise examined and found to be honeycombed with contradictions. Most of these I cannot go into. I must, however, touch upon one point—Mr. Bradley's attitude to the time-difficulty. All our thoughts about Nature imply time: the categories of Cause and Effect, of Substance or Accident, all that is implied by mechanism or by organism, is meaningless without it. Even our thinking itself has

duration. Consequently Mr. Bradley cannot adopt the easy way out of the difficulty according to which the self for which time-distinctions exist is itself "out of time." And yet the well-known Kantian antinomy—the difficulty of admitting either a first event or an endless series—remains unresolved. Mr. Bradley has added difficulties of his own. That which is in time cannot satisfy his criterion of reality, for it is ever passing away into something else, implies something else; in short, it is related, and therefore is not real. That which becomes is and is not. Its very being involves contradiction. The Absolute therefore must be out of time: time-distinctions must be somehow transcended in the Absolute. But Mr. Bradley frankly admits, as has not always been done by those who adopt such a position, that he does not in the least know of any kind of being which is out of time, and can attach no definite meaning to the language which he is compelled to use. The time-difficulty constitutes, therefore, one additional obstacle in the way of knowing Reality as it is, and in particular it is fatal to any attempt to discover the real or the Absolute in a self (as we understand self-hood), or any plurality of selves, for these are in time.

(4) I will not dwell on the ethical side of Mr. Bradley's doctrine, for it would lead us far from our subject, and I have dealt with it at length elsewhere. I will only say that in the contrast between the ideal of Self-development and the ideal of Self-sacrifice we are presented once more with that element of contradiction which penetrates all our knowledge. Thus Morality has to go the way of knowledge. Morality is self-contradictory, and therefore appearance only —not Reality or belonging to the Real except as inconsistent or self-contradictory appearances belong to the Real. We are therefore precluded from finding (with Kant) in the Practical Reason a new world, as it were, which is to redress the balance of the old —a practical truth which will serve humanity as a

212

substitute for the speculative truth which the limitations of our Reason have rendered impossible for us. In the Absolute, Mr. Bradley assures us—on what grounds he has omitted to explain except in so far as it constitutes part of his arbitrary definition of "the real"—all must be perfectly harmonious (the word here appears to be used in an ethical, and not a logical sense), and therefore must be very good. Our moral consciousness which pronounces that some things are very bad must therefore be a one-sided appearance. This apparent evil must in reality only add to the perfection and harmony of the whole. Our good and evil are only one-sided and contradictory appearances of a super-moral Absolute.

So far Mr. Bradley's argument might be said to have landed us in a position of pure Agnosticism— profounder than any ever dreamed of by Herbert Spencer and his kind. For Spencer's position was simply "*We* do not, and cannot know" the Absolute. Mr. Bradley's is "No being can know the Absolute, not even Himself or (as he prefers to say) itself." Mr. Spencer's position is "We cannot get at absolute truth": Mr. Bradley's is "there is no such thing as absolute truth; all truth is and must be partially false." But there is another side to Mr. Bradley's position, by which he goes near to reducing his most violent parodoxes to something very like platitude. Truth cannot be wholly true, and can never fully express the nature of reality: but not all truth is equally false. There are degrees of truth and degrees of Reality. Matter is not absolutely real, but it is not a mere delusion: the ideas of common life and of Science about Matter, though not absolutely true, contain a great deal of truth. Science is nearer to Reality than mere Common-sense. We approach still nearer the absolute truth of things when we adopt the Idealist's point of view, and look at matter in its due relation to mind. The Idealist is right in thinking the self more real than matter. The conception of God—as conceived of by Religion or Philosophy—brings us still nearer to the absolute Reality, for it represents an attempt to think of things as a whole. And in the whole there is more Reality than in the part. But still even the whole, considered as a whole, cannot be thought of as absolutely real, for the reasons already mentioned. The knowledge of common life, Science, Religion, Philosophy, represent stages or levels of knowledge, each of which brings us nearer absolute truth and absolute Reality than the one below it, though the goal which we are in search of is one which we can never actually reach: for the goal of absolute knowledge is one which would melt away for us in the very act of our reaching it. Absolute truth, if attained, would be no longer truth but Reality. Reality fully known would no longer be Reality.

How shall we examine this marvellous intellectual fabric? I think I can best do so by attempting to show that it involves a fundamental contradiction and inconsistency. That is, indeed, a difficult position to take up against Mr. Bradley: for the more contradictions one points out in knowledge—even in that latest and highest product of human knowledge constituted by Mr. Bradley's own system—the more his theory seems to be confirmed. You point out contradictions; he replies, " I told you so: the contradictions are necessary, and only prove my case—that all our knowledge involves contradictions, and that is just what I assert." Perhaps the best way of dealing with this position will be then to assume provisionally that Mr. Bradley is right, and ask ourselves only whether he has brought us as near to the truth about Reality as any system can do. For, though Mr. Bradley holds that contradictions in human knowledge are inevitable, he does not positively assert that contradictions are a mark of truth, such truth as it is possible for the human mind to obtain. He admits that we must provisionally assume the law of contra-

diction, and the other laws or categories of human
thought, and that at all events unnecessary and avoidable contradiction is a mark not merely of that limitation and consequent error to which all human thought
is doomed, but of avoidable error. I will ask then
whether Mr. Bradley has avoided such contradictions
in his ultimate *Weltanschauung*.

I will venture to say at once that there seems to
me to be in Mr. Bradley's system a fundamental and
irreconcilable contradiction between three sharply
opposed points of view. They may be conveniently
described as (1) Idealism, (2) Spinozism, (3)
Phenomenalism.

The side of Mr. Bradley's thought which meets us
first is Idealism; and this, I would venture to say,
constitutes the truest of those numerous selves which,
in accordance with Mr. Bradley's own teaching, I
shall take the liberty to attribute to him. "Sentient
experience is reality and what is not this is not real,"
"the real is nothing but experience," "everything is
experience": there we have the voice of the genuine
Idealist. But, when we are told to think of all the
kinds of conscious experience known to us as merely
adjectives of a substance which we do not know, when
this substance is spoken of as transcending the distinction between the thinker and the objects of his
thought, above all when we are invited to apply the
neuter pronoun to this substance instead of the mascu-
line, then I submit that Mr. Bradley has entered upon
the line of thought which conducts to Spinozism. It
is true that he does actually avoid Spinoza's conclusion; for, though he speaks of the Absolute as transcending the distinction between subject and object,
between thinker and the object thought of, he does
not speak of it as transcending the distinction between
mind and matter, or (to keep closer to Spinoza's
actual language) between Intelligence and Extension.
Mr. Bradley has no doubt that the Absolute is experience and he everywhere assumes that experience

means conscious experience. If he will not call the
Absolute " Mind," he definitely calls it " Spirit." But
I submit that he has no right to deny to the Absolute
all the characteristics of consciousness as we know
it—to deny to it the power of knowing either itself
or anything else, and still to call it consciousness or
experience. In justification of such a procedure,
Mr. Bradley appeals to that lowest form of consciousness in which feeling is not yet differentiated from
knowing, in which there is as yet no apprehended
contrast between self and not-self, in which there is
no distinction between logical subject and logical predicate. Of course he admits that this is a mere and
a distant analogy: he admits that he does not know
what such a not-knowing Consciousness is like. But
I submit that the analogy does not help us. To point
to the existence of a consciousness which is below
knowing does not help us to understand, or without
understanding to believe in, the existence of a consciousness which is above knowing, and yet (strange
to say) includes knowing. Mr. Bradley admits that
he can only supply us with an analogy. Yet he rejects the analogy of the self in thinking of the ultimate
Reality, and falls back upon the analogy of a much
lower kind of experience. He will urge of course that
the self will not do, because it implies the contrast
between self and not-self; and there we have relativity
at once. But he does not escape the difficulty by
treating the Absolute as a substance of which selves
are attributes, as a substantive of which they are
adjectives. For there too is relation. And if he
pleads that here again this relation of substance to
attribute is only intended as an analogy, I should
submit that the analogy is a particularly misleading
one. When we think of a substance, we necessarily
think either of a permanent self with changing conscious states, or of a material thing with changing
states known not to itself but to another mind. Mr.
Bradley will not allow us to think of the Absolute

after the analogy of a self: he therefore compels us practically to think of it after the analogy of a thing. Surreptitiously and unavowedly this is what he is doing when he talks of it as substance, or an " it," and, if, for reasons the force of which the Idealist cannot deny, this substance is not to be identified with matter as we know it, the logical outcome of this line of thought would be much better met by frankly dropping the assertion that the Absolute is consciousness, and saying with Spinoza that it is a substance which is neither mind nor matter, and of which both consciousness and extension are but attributes. But this of course would be to give up all that Mr. Bradley has said about the Absolute being experience, spirit, and the like, to give up, in fact, all his Idealism.

At this point Mr. Bradley would probably be disposed to accuse me of having forgotten another side of his system. Has he not warned us, more and more emphatically as he approaches the end of his book, that after all we are not to take too seriously his language about the Absolute? The Absolute is not to be taken as if it were something apart from its appearances: the Absolute in fact exists only *in* its appearances. Now, I submit, that here we are introduced to a third theory of the Universe, distinct from and irreconcilable with either of the other two. If after all there is no Absolute other than the appearances, what becomes of the fundamental distinction between the Reality and its appearances? Either we must say that the appearances are the Reality, or we must say that there is no Absolute but only appearances. The difference between these two ways of putting the matter will not be great: in either case we have really adopted the third view which I have ventured to describe as Phenomenalism. Of course Mr. Bradley will protest that, though in a sense nothing exists but appearances, it is not *as* appearances that they constitute the Absolute. It is not as a simple collection that they are the Absolute, but as a

Unity, as a system in which all have their place, and yet in which what is discordant or inconsistent in the appearances disappears. But still we cannot help asking what kind of existence has this Unity or system? If there is any mind for which it exists as a system, then it would seem that after all the Reality must be a Mind (or minds) which knows the system, and can be distinguished from it, whatever difficulties may remain in understanding the character of its relation to other minds. In the earlier parts of *Appearance and Reality* it would seem as if Mr. Bradley did on the whole believe that there is a mind or an experience in which all other minds or centres of consciousness were in some sense included and merged, and yet which was more than they. The Absolute, we are assured, is not merely One, not merely one system, but one experience, an eternal experience, an individual experience. If the Absolute " perhaps strictly does not feel pleasure," " that is only because it has something in which pleasure is included " (p. 534). Such statements imply consciousness and a consciousness distinguishable from each and every finite subject. It possesses a sense of humour of a rather malicious type; it can enjoy a practical joke.[1] But as we go on, we meet with such utterances as these: " Outside of finite experience there is neither a natural world nor any other world at all " (p. 279). " The Absolute . . . has no assets beyond appearances " (p. 489). " There is no reality at all anywhere except in appearance, and in our appearance we can discern the main nature of Reality " (p. 550). And in a recent article in *Mind* Mr. Bradley has asserted more unequivocally than ever that he does " not believe in any reality outside of and apart from the totality of finite mind." [2] Now I submit that this is really a third view of Reality absolutely inconsistent with either of the two others

[1] Ibid., p. 194.
[2] *Mind*, N.S. vol. xvi (1907), p.179.

—inconsistent with an inconsistency far more absolute and irreconcilable than he has ever alleged in the
thinking of poor common-sense, of " popular " Philosophy, or of orthodox Theologies. It practically
amounts to the assertion that the collective conscious
experience of the Universe is the Reality. " Yes,"
Mr. Bradley will reply, " but not as such, not as a mere
collection. For so considered they are inhar-
monious; they contradict themselves; and contradiction is the note of Unreality." But, I would insist,
in what Mind or by what Mind is this process of
reconciling and absorbing and removing the contradictions of Appearance performed? " By finite
minds," he will reply, " so far as men of Science at a
lower level and Philosophers at a higher level actually
succeed in performing this process." Since Mr.
Bradley is (I suppose) the only Philosopher who has
excogitated exactly this conception of such an all-
comprehensive and all-reconciling experience, the
natural tendency of such a line of thought would be
to make out that Mr. Bradley alone, or Mr. Bradley
and his disciples, are the Absolute. But after all
Mr. Bradley admits that no human mind or minds
ever can perfectly and in detail perform this process of
perfect reconciliation, absorption, removal of contradictions, transcending of relations. Then in what sense
does an experience in which this remarkable feat is
performed really exist? To say that it exists and
yet does not enter into any consciousness whatever
involves a flat contradiction of all that Mr. Bradley
has said against the possibility of Reality being a something which is not conscious, and of which no one is
conscious. It is to give up the whole idealistic side
of his teaching. If it exists neither in any consciousness nor out of any consciousness, it becomes a mere
ideal of a kind of consciousness admitted to be unattainable, and it is absurd to describe such a non-exis-
tent as experience. The appearances as they appear
—with all their contradictions and inconsistencies,

except in so far as any finite Philosopher has succeeded in removing them—are left as the only
reality.

Of course in Mr. Bradley's own writings these contradictions are disguised by many ingenious devices.
The plausibility of his position consists in a see-saw
between the two—or rather the three—views of
Reality. When he exposes the difficulties of rival
systems, his own system appears to escape them by
the assurance that " somehow " (Mr. Bradley's system
might be described as the Philosophy of a " Somehow "), all these contradictions are reconciled in the
Absolute. When faced with the difficulty of a view
which makes Reality consist in so strange an experience, an experience which does not know itself and
yet in which all knowledge is absorbed, in which there
is no relation or consciousness of relation and yet in
which all relations have their being which includes
all things and yet in which there is no plurality (for
plurality is relation), then Mr. Bradley exhibits the
other side of his shield and says, " Oh, but this Absolute is only in the experiences: it is nothing apart from
them or even beyond them." But the two positions
absolutely refuse to come together. We are assured
that they come together somehow in the Absolute.
But if our minds are to be allowed any power whatever of judging about the nature of the Reality, they
cannot come together even in the Absolute. If Contradiction is the note of appearance or unreality, then
Mr. Bradley's Absolute is itself the most unreal of
all appearances, the greatest unreality in this world
of shams. To tell us that all these distinctive, one-
sided appearances may be harmonised in a complete
experience might be intelligible; to say that they
actually are harmonised in a consciousness and that
that consciousness is the Reality might be intelligible.
At least that might seem intelligible to some persons,
though I personally could only admit the intelligi-
bility in the sense in which one can admit the intelli-

gibility of propositions which seem to one absurd. But to tell us that these self-contradictory appearances actually are such an harmonious and reconciling experience, while at the same time no consciousness exists except the self-contradictory appearances, is simply to require us to make an act of faith which cannot be made without such a sacrifice of the intellect as no religious fanatic or infallible Pontiff has ever demanded. If nothing is real but experience, a system of which no one is conscious cannot be Reality. If the unthought of, unexperienced system is Reality, Reality is something outside consciousness, and then on that view it is not true that " Reality is experience." Mr. Bradley has mistaken for Reality an ideal of knowledge—an ideal towards which, as he contends, all our efforts to know point as to a goal, but which, according to his own admission, could not be attained, which does not exist in consciousness anywhere, and which (if it were attained) would cease to be knowledge.

I shall now have the temerity to point out in a more positive way the fundamental mistake which, as it seems to me, lies at the bottom of Mr. Bradley's difficulties. I have nothing to say against that part of his argument which shows the impossibility of treating matter as by itself real. Of course matter has its own reality: it is only when it is taken out of its proper relation to consciousness that it becomes unreal. Its reality is that of actual or possible experience. To develop this fully would occupy much time. It is enough to say that here I am on common idealistic ground—the ground which, so far, Mr. Bradley shares with all thoroughgoing Idealists: nor have I any objection to enter against his criticism of the common Hegelian attempts to get rid of or practically to ignore the element which feeling undoubtedly contributes to the building up of what we call material things. It is this insistence in which I for one should discover Mr. Bradley's most conspicuous service to philosophical progress. But when we come to actual conscious experience, it seems to me that the suggestion that any such experience can be unreal is completely unmeaning. I recognise that that particular kind of mental experience which we call thought or knowledge is not all equally true. I have learned from Mr. Bradley the lesson that knowledge, though built up of perceptual material, is not the same thing as actual perception: it represents a manipulation, as it were, of our immediate experience. And our first efforts at this co-ordination are undoubtedly full of mistake, imperfection, one-sidedness, sometimes actual contradiction. It is the business of each successive stage in the development of thought to get rid of the inconsistency or one-sidedness in the preceding. It is undeniable, too, that *our* thought at least accomplishes this task only at the cost of getting in a sense away from the actual reality of things: it aims at representing what we perceive, but it only succeeds in doing this by leaving out much of the truth. Some of the incoherences and contradictions pointed out by Mr. Bradley may be really there. I will assume for the moment that they are all there. But, whatever may be said about the inadequate truth which can be claimed for that element in our consciousness which is called knowledge, nothing that may be said on this head can possibly affect its reality when considered simply as an actual conscious experience. No matter what manipulation some crude experience of ours may undergo before it passes into knowledge, the crude experience actually occurred before it was so manipulated. The raw material had, so to speak, as much reality as the finished article. Conscious states as they are actually experienced, are perfectly real: knowledge and even false knowledge or error are real. There may be degrees of Reality, if by that is meant that different kinds of consciousness possess different degrees of insight into their own natures or the nature of other knowable realities, or again in the sense that

222

they may possess different degrees of value. But this is, on the whole, as it seems to me, a misleading way of speaking. In strictness the most passing thrill of immediate feeling is no less real than the highest moments of philosophic insight in the soul of a Plato. One state of mind may, considered as knowledge, come nearer the truth about Reality than another, but considered as so much psychical experience it is just so much and no more a part of Reality. Everything, as Professor Bosanquet has put it, is real, so long as it does not pretend to be anything but what it is. The unreality only comes in when it is taken by a knowing mind to be more or other than it is. And that is best expressed by saying that there are degrees of truth, but no degrees of Reality.

And from this there must follow a further consequence. All speculations about lower kinds of consciousness being swallowed up or combined in a higher kind of consciousness must be dismissed as evolving unthinkable contradictions. I have for instance a certain experience on the strength of which I judge a sensation to be related to another sensation—related, say, in the way of posteriority. You may tell me that that notion is from the point of view of higher knowledge a mistake, for there can be no relations in reality, and the relation between the relative and its relation is unthinkable. Another mind, or my own at a later date, may see this sensation and relation transfigured into a unity in which the distinction between sensation and relation disappears. Let us assume that this may be the case. But that will not alter the fact that I made the mistake. The mental experience was just what it was, not something else. The mental experience of making a mistake can never be swallowed up or merged in an experience which involves no mistake : mental confusion is a reality which can never be transmuted into an experience in which all is clear, consistent, and " harmonious." An experience in which that distinction is "transcended" is not the same experience as mine. "Everything," as Bishop Butler put it, is "what it is and not another thing." I am bound to accuse Mr. Bradley of not having duly learned the simple lesson taught by this (in comparison with such thinkers as himself) simple-minded Georgian Bishop.

What then will be the effect of this contention, if admitted, upon our ultimate *Weltanschauung*? I do not deny that knowledge does postulate as its ideal a system of coherent truth, though many of the assumptions about the nature of this system are, I hold, quite gratuitous assumptions. The mere hypothesis that we make for the purposes of scientific investigation or reasoning may be far from possessing that absolute and unvariable truthfulness which we erroneously attribute to them. But that the Universe must form, or that there is reason to believe that it does form, an ordered system of some kind, I fully admit—though philosophers are far too ready to make innumerable assumptions as to the nature of what is meant by order and system. Still, I should contend that we must not identify any fabric of coherent truth with Reality. Scientific knowledge exists as a fact in certain consciousnesses. There may exist a knowledge which surpasses in its completeness and coherence what we call knowledge as much as the knowledge of Science or Philosophy surpasses that of common, unanalysed, unreflecting experience. But quite equally, side by side with this knowledge, there exists unscientific knowledge, error, mistake, confusion; raw, crude, sensible experience. All these must be included in the whole: no piece of conscious experience can ever be banished from the realm of reality, or ever become, for a mind that truly knows, other than it was. Complete knowledge would have to know what all this experience was, but without being it. To know what another thinks, or feels, or wills, or otherwise experiences, is not the same thing as to be or to have that experience. Reality then consists of all the actual conscious experience that there is, was, or will be. An experience in which contradictions and one-sidedness should have disappeared, or been swallowed up, or transformed into something else would not be the whole. A knowledge in which they appeared to be so transmuted could not be true knowledge of the whole.

But of course we cannot think of this world of experience simply as a succession of experiences. In our own conscious experience the successive moments of thought, emotion, perception present themselves as happening to a continuous, relatively permanent self: and we have reason to infer some similar, though inferior kind of connection and continuity in the experience even of those inferior minds to which we cannot reasonably attribute self-consciousness as it exists in ourselves. Some degree of continuity is a matter of immediate experience in ourselves: and it is a necessity of thought to assume that any experience which begins to be must be regarded as ultimately an effect or product of a something which is permanent. The fleeting experience in time, though real, cannot be regarded as the whole of Reality. For our provisional account of the real as all the conscious experience of the Universe we must therefore substitute all the conscious beings that there are—not taken, of course, in abstraction from their successive experiences but with those experiences. The real world is made up of conscious Spirits and their experiences.

But of what sort are those Spirits, and how many are there? Can we think of the spirits of men and animals and similarly limited intelligences as constituting the ultimate Reality? It is an obvious necessity of thought that something must have existed from all eternity. We can as little treat a mere succession of temporary selves generating one another as being by themselves the whole Reality as a mere succession of experiences not united together and forming the experience of one and the same Spirit.

P

Something must persist throughout the changes, some reality on which the changes are dependent. Now if we assume on the ordinary idealistic grounds that nothing can possess in the fullest sense real and independent existence but conscious Spirits, the eternal Reality which is the source of all other Reality must be thought of as either one Spirit or many co-eternal spirits. The prima facie view of the matter is that spirits such as ours have not always existed. If they did, there is no reason to suppose that even between them they know the whole world which there was to be known. Geology tells us of a world which existed before us: even if we existed in some other state, there is no reason to assume that we formerly knew the geological history of their planet while that history was being enacted. Yet if that world existed, and the existence of material things implies experience, all of it must have entered in some way into the experience of one Spirit or more. All that has been said by Mr. Bradley and others as to the necessity of thinking that the world must form a coherent unity is in favour of supposing that the whole of it is known to one Mind, and is not merely the collective experience of many minds, each of which knows it in part, none of it as a whole.

If the world is to have any existence as a system or unity, it must exist in and for the experience of One Mind—one Mind at least. The hypothesis of a plurality of omniscient Minds is not, indeed, absolutely self-contradictory. Such a hypothesis might be dismissed as gratuitous, even if we thought of these Minds as merely knowing the world. But directly we introduce the idea of Will into our conception of the relation between the world and the minds whose experience it ultimately is, the hypothesis of two or more omniscient Minds becomes impossible. I have not time now to develop the argument that Causality or activity is intelligible only as the will of a Conscious being. My present hearers will of course

226

know where that line of thought has been developed. I will only remind them in passing that Kant may now be numbered among the adherents of that view —a view which involves the cancelling and suppression of two-thirds of his Critique and of much more that his disciples have based upon it.[1] I must be content here with saying that the unity, intercommunion, and system of the Universe prove that, if it was willed by Mind at all, it was willed by One Mind. The hypothesis of two or more minds which by their joint and completely concordant volitions continuously keep in being one and the same world of Nature and of other Spirits can hardly require serious refutation. It involves the hypothesis of a pre-established harmony which is not pre-established and which is harmonious only by accident. In the absence of such a grotesque alternative, we are driven to the view that Reality consists of all the Spirits that there are, among which only One is eternal and omniscient, and the source or ground of all the rest.

It will be obvious that I have now frankly taken leave of the definition of Reality adopted by Mr. Bradley himself. That definition seems to me an absolutely arbitrary one. This Reality which excludes all relation is after all the old " One " of Parmenides, upon the emptiness and vanity of which all subsequent Philosophy has been a comment. An Absolute which excludes all relation is simply a One without a Many. To talk about a One which somehow " includes " many members without being related to any of them and without their being related to one another is simply to take back with one phrase what has been conceded by another. Inclusion is after all for our thought a relation, and we have no other thoughts by which to think. The result of this quest has been what might have been anticipated. It has turned out that the One has no real existence except in so far as it is a name for the many consi-

[1] James Ward, *Naturalism and Agnosticism*, II, p. 191.

dered in their mutual relations. Mr. Bradley's Absolute has turned out to be, as Green said of the search for a Real which was behind and independent of consciousness, simply that of which nothing can be said. Of course, if by Reality is meant the whole of Reality, such a Reality cannot have relation to anything outside itself: as to internal relations, there is no reason whatever for supposing that Reality, taken in its ordinary significance, involves any such exclusion.

Of course Mr. Bradley would reply that he has given reasons for holding that the notion of relativity involves incoherences and inconsistencies which we cannot suppose to belong to ultimately real things. The difficulty is one which would demand as elaborate an examination as Mr. Bradley has himself given it. Here I can but briefly urge two points. First, I would submit that, even if he had succeeded in making good all—and even more than all—the contradictions which he has attempted to discover in our intellectual categories, that would only go to show what I for one should never deny—that is to say, the inadequacy of our thoughts about Reality. Mr. Bradley admits that he is obliged to use these categories of human thought. His own theory of Reality depends for whatever plausibility it possesses upon a use of these categories. In so far as he does make any attempt at getting beyond them, he only involves himself in more and far more glaring contradictions than those which he seeks to avoid. Our modes of thought, when we are most consistent and when we seem to ourselves to be most reasonable, may be inadequate and imperfect modes of thinking; but we are not likely to get nearer the truth by indulging in what seems self-contradictory even to us. There may be unavoidable contradictions in our thought: that is a poor reason for introducing avoidable ones. That which seems absurd to us is not likely to seem less so to the Absolute. And therefore, even if we suppose that the idea of relation in general—or the relation

228

of whole and part in particular—is inadequate to the nature of Reality, the idea of a relationless Reality or (what is the same thing) of a whole without any parts at all is likely to be still more so. Mr. Bradley's device of throwing all contradictions into the Absolute and pronouncing that they are somehow reconciled in and for the Absolute is just as much open to believers in another kind of Absolute. Indeed, an Absolute which is thought of as consisting in self-conscious Spirits—in many reproductions or imperfect Incarnations of a single self-consciousness which is also omniscient—would seem to be distinctly more capable of such feats than an Absolute which is correctly described by an "it," whose maximum intelligence is represented, or (so far as Mr. Bradley's system goes) *may be* represented, by such minds as ours, and which after all only exists in those admittedly self-contradictory appearances.

But secondly I must confess that the difficulties upon which Mr. Bradley insists with regard to relation do not much appeal to me. I do, indeed, recognise that the experience which is attributed to God cannot be exactly like our experience: there cannot be in it the same distinction between abstract knowledge on the one hand—based on that process of generalising which, as Mr. Bradley has shown us, leaves out so much of the perceptual Reality—and actual sensation on the other, which as it approaches the state of pure sensation becomes increasingly exclusive of thought. "Somehow," to use Mr. Bradley's favourite adverb, we must suppose that in God there is not this distinction between abstract knowledge and actual perception; so far I recognise the high value of Mr. Bradley's criticism upon the Hegelian attempt to make the thought of God, and so the reality of the world, identical with our system of abstract universals to the avowed or implied exclusion of all that wealth of actual perception to which these Universals owe all their content and all their claim to hold good

of, or represent, Reality. But, if we cannot suppose
that God's knowledge consists like ours in abstract
universals, got by the clumsy process of generalising
from isolated perceptions, this is not because such
knowledge implies relations but because it implies an
advance from the unknown to the known, and so pre-
supposes ignorance. Moreover, such knowledge,
even when attained, fails to express the whole truth
of actual perception: while actual perception, so long
and so far as it is *mere* perception, does not know even
itself. Such a distinction between the " what " and the
" that " (as Mr. Bradley calls it) is impossible to an
Omniscient Mind. The experience of the divine
Mind must somehow transcend this distinction between a thought which falls short of Reality and a
reality which falls short of thought. But I see
no reason to believe that the element of Relation
must disappear from such a consciousness, though
for it relation may well become something other and
more than it is for us. I cannot acknowledge the
alleged self-contradictoriness of Relation. I do not
see that, because we think of one sensation as related
to another sensation, we therefore require a new relation to express the relation between the sensation and
the relation, and so on *ad infinitum.* So to argue
implies that we think of the relation as being an
existence apart from that which is related, and that
is inconsistent with the nature of a relation: just as,
when with Plato—the Plato of certain dialogues or
certain moments—we treat a universal as a real thing
apart from its particulars, we are really taking away
from it all that belongs to the nature of a universal,
making it into a fresh particular, and exposing ourselves to the familiar τρίτος ἄνθρωπος criticism of
Aristotle. A relation which itself wanted a relation
to hook it on to its term would not be a relation
at all. This difficulty—and many other difficulties of
Mr. Bradley—seem to me simply to be created by the
transparent device of taking ultimate notions, and de-

manding that they shall be explained. It is just like asking *why* two and two should make four, or asking *in what* consists the equality of the two angles at the base of an isosceles triangle, or demanding a definition of redness which shall explain the notion to a man blind from his birth, or insisting that, if one part of space is connected with the adjoining part, there must be a link to connect them which we must be able to isolate from the adjoining space and hand round for inspection. There must be a limit to all explanation, and when we have analysed the objects of perception into a sensuous content and certain intellectual relations, we have reached that limit. I do not deny that an omniscient mind may know more about the matter than we do; but even in relations as we know them there is no contradiction.

Among the many consequences which follow from the rejection of Mr. Bradley's views about relation, there is one which calls in our present connection for special notice. If relatedness or two-ness is not a mark of unreality, there is no reason why we should assume that in the Absolute the distinction between subject and object must altogether disappear. No doubt we can look upon the subject or subjects and the nature which they know as together constituting a single Reality. If the word Absolute is to be used at all, we must say that the Absolute includes the subject or subjects together with the Nature which is, in the most ultimate analysis, the experience of those subjects. In so far as subject and object are each of them unreal and unintelligible without the other, we may no doubt, if we like, speak of a " higher Unity " which transcends the distinction; but we must not think of this higher Unity as a special and different Being with a nature or characteristics of its own distinct from the nature of subject and object considered as related to and implying each other. A further consequence of rejecting Mr. Bradley's Anti-relationism will be that we shall have cut away all

ground for treating the distinction between one self
and another—between one human self and another, or
between any human self and that divine Self which we
have seen to be logically implied in the existence of the
world—as in any way an unreal distinction which
has got to be merged and transcended in the Absolute.
And this will avoid some of the outrageous positions
to which Mr. Bradley would commit us. An omniscient experience which should include in itself experiences which are not omniscient involves a contradiction. And we are told that in the Absolute there
must be no contradiction. An omniscient Being
could not have the particular experience which consists in not being omniscient. He might know what
such a limited experience is, but it would not be his
experience or be known as such.

While we recognise the differences between
thought, feeling, experience and all other words expressive of consciousness as they are for and in God
from what they are in ourselves, while we admit that,
in the scholastic phrase, such expressions are used
sensu eminentiori, we need not make the difference
to be so great as is implied in the assertion that in the
divine experience all distinction between subject and
object disappears—a mode of representation which is
apt to end in a virtual evaporation of all real meaning
in the assertion that God is Spirit or Mind and to
embark upon the road by which a nominal Idealism
so often descends into the virtual Naturalism of
Spinoza. At the same time we shall be able to avoid
what seems to me the excessive subjectivism of Mr.
Bradley's extremist idealistic utterances. If relation
is not to be expelled from Reality, we need no more
merge the object in the subject than the subject in
the object. I do not reject Mr. Bradley's phrase
"nothing exists but experience," but the phrase, taken
by itself and still 'more when taken in connection
with Mr. Bradley's attitude towards relations, may
easily be taken to mean that it is an experience in

which all distinction between a consciousness of objects in space and non-spatial experiences such as emotions (though after all even these are vaguely localised) is altogether lost and denied. We need not deny the reality of things because we assert they could not exist apart from consciousness.

A certain community of Nature we must, again, recognise between God and all lesser spirits, a community great in proportion to the level of each spirit's capacities and achievements. But community is not identity. The Unity that we are in search of does not exclude differences. All these Spirits together no doubt make a single Reality, but the unity which they possess is not the particular kind of Unity which we recognise in ourselves as constituting self-consciousness or personality. God may no doubt reasonably be supposed to possess that Unity in Himself carried to a degree of which personality in us gives us only a glimpse. But to distinguish oneself from other Spirits, however fully one may know them, is not (as some people seem to imagine) an imperfection or (in any derogatory sense) a limitation, but, on the contrary, a note of the highest level to which Being can attain. It represents an ideal, to which other consciousnesses approximate in proportion to their intellectual elevation, and to which the nearest approach known to us is constituted by the human intelligence at its highest.

I have passed over a host of difficulties. A host of the alleged difficulties, contradictions, and incoherences in human knowledge have been left unexamined. I can only say here that some of them appear to me to be imaginary, others greatly exaggerated; while others remain real and undeniable, and consequently set a limit to the completeness and adequacy of our knowledge, though they do not, as it seems to me, involve the inferences which Mr. Bradley draws from them.

These matters I must pass over, but there is one of

233

these alleged contradictions about which a word must be said even in the most summary criticism of Mr. Bradley's position. Green's timeless individual self he has dismissed in a contemptuous paragraph: he still believes in a timeless Absolute. I am far from denying that there are antinomies involved in our ideas of time, and I do not believe that any thinker has ever transcended them: certainly they are not transcended by merely saying " Let them be reconciled where all other contradictions are reconciled—in the Absolute." But the contradictions are not as great as Mr. Bradley makes them. The mere fact that time involves relativity and therefore multiplicity does not involve the reduction of time to the level of appearance. With the rejection of the notion that relativity is equivalent to unreality, we shall have got rid of one of Mr. Bradley's main reasons for treating time as unreal. But there remains the fundamental antinomy—the impossibility of believing either in a first event or in an infinite series of real events. This does not warrant our calling time unreal. Empty time is of course unreal, but temporality enters into all our experience and is an element in our experience as real as anything we know or can conceive. To talk of God or of the Absolute or ultimate Reality as timeless is to use language which can mean nothing to us, or rather language which is certainly false. Whatever be the true solution of the difficulties involved in the nature of time, we shall not diminish them by denying the reality of an element in actual experience which is as real as any other element in the most real thing we know or can conceive.

I will not develop these considerations any further, for two reasons. In the first place the question of time is the most difficult question of Metaphysics, and any approach to a serious criticism of Mr. Bradley's treatment of it would be wholly beyond the limits which I have designed for this paper. And in the second place much has already been done in the way of protest against the cheap and easy attempts to transcend the time-antinomy which were in vogue not many years ago. Without mentioning others, it will be enough to say that I recognise this as one of the most permanent and valuable elements in the philosophy of M. Bergson. Whatever becomes of his system as a whole, M. Bergson's insistence on the reality of experience as seen from the inside, and on change and temporality as inherent elements in that reality, has I think, supplied just the criticism which Mr. Bradley's attitude towards time demands, although there may be not an equal insistence on the complementary principle that change implies something permanent.

I have no disposition to deny the reality or the gravity of some of the difficulties about time, but the moral which I should draw from them is different from Mr. Bradley's. The general conclusion of his whole argument is that, though everything is appearance, yet " in our appearance we can discover the main nature of reality." If it were true that the Absolute is out of time, while the appearances are all in time, it certainly could not be said that we could discover the main nature of Reality from the appearances. The difference between an existence in time and an existence out of time is so fundamental, so abysmal, that it is difficult to say what the one could have in common with the other. Mr. Bradley is, as it appears to me, too sceptical in his premisses, much too dogmatic in his conclusions. He is too sceptical about the validity of our knowledge in its parts; he is too unwarrantably confident and dogmatic in his assertions about the Universe as a whole. The difficulties which he insists upon about time do not warrant the assertion that the Absolute is out of time, or that time-distinctions are purely subjective or in any sense unreal. But they do warrant the assertion that we do not and cannot understand fully the nature of time, and consequently cannot fully understand the nature of ultimate Reality. Till this difficulty is removed, the pretentious systems, Hegelian or other, which professed to explain all difficulties and to give full and complete insight into the ultimate nature of things are doomed to failure. But I believe it is possible to show that a system which takes time and things in time as we find them and treats them, notwithstanding the difficulties, as real and objective is in all probability nearer the reality than any of those which ignore or pretend to explain them away— nearer the absolute truth speculatively and still more so when treated as imperfect and inadequate representations of Reality for the purposes of life and practice.

There are aspects of Mr. Bradley's chameleon-like system which would enable it to be represented as merely amounting to such an assertion of the inadequacy of our knowledge which is nevertheless sufficient to supply us with guidance through life. Much in it might fit in with a system of thought which accepted the primacy of the Practical Reason. But his distrust of the Moral Consciousness prevents our looking at it in this light. That is precluded by his admission that we have to assume in practice moral distinctions which we know speculatively to be not only inadequate but false. For one who believes that our moral consciousness gives us the fullest glimpses of insight into the nature of Reality that we possess, the mere fact that his system condemns us to adopt this attitude of ethical scepticism, supplies by itself a considerable presumption against its speculative truth.

The question of time is not the only direction in which I recognise that Mr. Bradley has performed good service in pointing out the inadequacy of our knowledge, and undermining the philosophies which tend to conceal this fact by substituting imposing rhetoric for thought. There is at least some truth in Mr. Bradley's doctrine that in a sense we cannot know anything perfectly without knowing the whole. It is, as it seems to me, an exaggeration to say that this implies that all our knowledge is partial error: for sometimes—as, for instance, in Arithmetic and Geometry—we can see immediately that all further knowledge must be irrelevant to the accuracy of the particular truth which we grasp when we pronounce, for instance, that two and two make four. In mathematics abstraction is so complete that we know that here abstraction involves no error. But that is decreasingly the case as Science becomes more concrete, and the maxim attains its maximum truth as the highest objects of knowledge are reached. Above all, with regard to our knowledge of God, it is most undoubtedly true that our knowledge must be inadequate, that nothing short of complete knowledge of the Universe and every part of it could give us complete and adequate knowledge, and here it may well be true that every proposition that we can lay down may be to some extent infected with error on account of the inadequate and partial character of our knowledge. Here we have no immediate knowledge that what we know not could not modify the inferences that we draw from what we do know. Our knowledge may be sufficient for practical guidance—not merely for actual conduct, but also for religious emotion, and faith, and aspiration. If Pragmatism would only limit itself to insisting upon this inadequacy, and upon the importance of the knowledge which guides life as compared with mere speculation, instead of substituting wilful caprice for the use of our Reason up to the point to which its powers enable us to penetrate, I could recognise its influence on Philosophy as a wholesome one: but, because our brightest guide through the darkness of this world is but a rushlight, that seems to me a poor reason for blowing it out, and insisting on walking blindly and unnecessarily in the dark.

Whether our knowledge is sufficient for practical

guidance and for the support of those religious beliefs and aspirations which so powerfully influence practice, depends mainly upon the confidence which we repose in the Practical Reason. Perhaps in order that this paper may not be more incomplete than it is I may be allowed briefly to repeat the criticism which I have elsewhere elaborated. I believe it to be possible to show that Mr. Bradley's discovery of a fundamental contradiction in our practical Reason is a sheer *ignis fatuus*. Our moral consciousness does not say that all self-development and all self-sacrifice are right (that would be a contradiction): it does not even say that *all* self-development and *all* self-sacrifice are good; if it did, there would be no contradiction there.[1] It does tell us that *some* self-contradiction and *some* self-sacrifice are good, and (difficult of course as such questions are in practice) it is not unequal to the task of balancing one good against another, and of seeking to realise an ideal of human life in which both self-development and self-sacrifice shall have their due and proper place. It is always right to aim at the greatest good; though there is no contradiction in saying that one good can sometimes only be attained by the sacrifice of another. And if our Practical Reason involves no such contradiction, there is no ground for distrusting it, any more than for distrusting our scientific reasoning, in spite of the obvious fallibility of any particular individual mind, and the inadequacy of all human knowledge. If our moral consciousness is not to be trusted, we have no right to use moral categories at all in our theory of the Universe, and Mr. Bradley has no right to say that good is an attribute of the real while evil is merely appearance. If our judgements of value are to be trusted, we have no reason for doubting that for the Mind and Will which is the source of all Reality this ideal is as valid as for us.

[1] I have dealt with this point at length in my *Theory of Good and Evil*, II, 85 sq., 268 sq.

There is no reason for attributing to God a different Morality (as regards its fundamental principles) than that which we recognise as applicable to human conduct, any more than for supposing that for God quantity and number are essentially different from that recognised by the purely human affair which we call Arithmetic.

And if our moral consciousness is to be trusted as an inadequate revelation of the Divine—two things must follow. First, we may and must think of the Divine Will as morally good, and directed towards the greatest attainable realisation of what presents itself to the Moral Consciousness as the highest good. Secondly, we cannot think of a Universe in which our Moral Consciousness pronounces that there is much evil as perfectly good. The evil exists, though (if our moral ideas contain any revelation of the Divine) it can only exist for the sake of the good. The series of events which make up the world's history is directed towards the good. But the good is not fully realised yet. How much good is destined to be realised, we cannot tell. Enough for us to know two things: (1) that enough good will be realised to justify its being willed by a righteous and all-wise Mind, (2) that our co-operation is required in realising it. And this is all that is necessary to justify religious faith and to inspire moral effort.